MW01087701

A MORE PERFECT PARTY

A MORE PERFECT PARTY

THE NIGHT *SHIRLEY CHISHOLM* AND *DIAHANN CARROLL* RESHAPED POLITICS

JUANITA TOLLIVER

LEGACY LIT

New York

Legacy Lit
Hachette Book Group
1290 Avenue of the Americas
New York, NY 10104
LegacyLitBooks.com
@LegacyLitBooks

First Edition: January 2025

Legacy Lit is an imprint of Grand Central Publishing. The Legacy Lit name and logo are registered trademarks of Hachette Book Group, Inc.

The publisher is not responsible for websites (or their content) that are not owned by the publisher.

The Hachette Speakers Bureau provides a wide range of authors for speaking events. To find out more, go to hachettespeakersbureau.com or email HachetteSpeakers@hbgusa.com.

Legacy Lit books may be purchased in bulk for business, educational, or promotional use. For information, please contact your local bookseller or the Hachette Book Group Special Markets Department at special.markets@hbgusa.com.

Print book interior design by Amy Quinn.

Library of Congress Cataloging-in-Publication Data

Names: Tolliver, Juanita, author.
Title: A more perfect party : the night Shirley Chisholm and Diahann Carroll reshaped politics / Juanita Tolliver.
Description: First edition. | New York : Legacy Lit, 2025. | Includes bibliographical references.
Identifiers: LCCN 2024035490 | ISBN 9781538770221 (hardcover) | ISBN 9781538770245 (ebook)
Subjects: LCSH: Chisholm, Shirley, 1924-2005. | Carroll, Diahann—Political activity. | African American women politicians. | African Americans—Politics and government. | Democratic Party (U.S.)—History—20th century. | Political participation—Social aspects—United States.
Classification: LCC E840.8.C48 T65 2025 | DDC 328.73/092 [B]—dc23 /eng/20240918
LC record available at https://lccn.loc.gov/2024035490

ISBNs: 978-1-5387-7022-1 (hardcover), 978-1-5387-7024-5 (ebook)

Printed in the United States of America

LSC

Printing 1, 2024

For my granddad, Arzell, and my niece, Amaya.
You are the bookends of my world.

CONTENTS

INTRODUCTION Shirley Chisholm Called It 1
ONE The Party 11
TWO The Money 25
THREE The Activist 43
FOUR The Youth 63
FIVE The Media 79
SIX The Celebrity Influence 101
SEVEN The (White) Feminists 121
EIGHT The Sisterhood 141
NINE The Legacy 165
CONCLUSION The Power 179

Bibliography and Sources *189*
Acknowledgments *209*

A MORE PERFECT PARTY

INTRODUCTION

SHIRLEY CHISHOLM CALLED IT

"Black women have had to develop a larger vision of our society than perhaps any other group... When black women win victories, it is a boost for virtually every segment of society."

—Angela Davis, *Women, Race, and Class*

"DID YOU EVER THINK *THIS COUNTRY*, IN 2024, WOULD BE here?"

By April 2024, I had been providing on-air political analysis for NBC and MSNBC for five years, having worked my way up from an occasional guest to an official analyst for the network. The bulk of my work included sharing data-driven insights with the network's hosts and millions of daily viewers, and at times I went so far as to challenge the assumptions embedded within the hosts' questions. This particular segment was on the Arizona Supreme Court's decision to uphold an 1864 law to ban abortion, and the host opened by emphasizing the context of the era. "Abe Lincoln had just been re-elected in 1864. Arizona wasn't even a state...Women didn't have the right to vote." While she stated these facts to draw attention to the seemingly anachronistic decision from the state court, I rejected her framing of surprise and horror because this decision *did*, in fact, fit with the battle for reproductive rights happening more than 150 years later.

Having worked in and around Democratic politics for more than a decade before transitioning to my present work in media, I have led advocacy initiatives and mobilizations against the long-standing effort by Republicans to overturn *Roe v. Wade* and ban abortions through the courts and Republican-controlled state legislatures. I understood the GOP's game when it came to snatching away our most basic freedoms. I also understood that Democrats never seized the opportunity to codify abortion rights as federal law, even when they controlled the White House, the US Senate, and the House of Representatives. All of this context and awareness informed my approach during this particular segment, and it precipitated my challenge to the premise of the question being asked.

"Yes," I replied matter-of-factly. The host was visibly shocked. "Republicans have been pushing for us to be here for years," I continued, providing verbal receipts that supported my assertion. "Every time Donald Trump beats his chest and claims that he single-handedly overturned *Roe v. Wade*, that cleared the way for bans like this and the ban that we saw the Florida Supreme court… [uphold] last week." She paused, blinked slowly, and shuffled her notes as my analysis sank in.

As the show wrapped, I anticipated what my granddad would say when he called to talk about the segment, as had become our custom.

I was always happy when my grandfather caught my on-air segments, even though I never tell my family when I will be appearing on live television. It's just one of my anxious and often futile attempts at limiting the variables tumbling through my mind while I'm at work. My anxiety is also why I wear a uniform of black clothing, curls swept to one side, and a deep red lipstick for every single television appearance. That way I can focus all of my energy on the chaotic news cycle and my own substantive political analysis. Granddad's lucky streak of seeing me on-air is largely attributed to the fact that he leaves his television on MSNBC with the volume level just below 80.

My granddad has been a reassuring, loving, and understanding figure in my life for as long as I can remember. He has consistently calmed my concerns about career changes and life transitions by reminding me of how far I have come. He even keeps a printed copy of my LinkedIn profile hanging on his refrigerator. Since childhood, he and I would spend many predawn hours discussing history, politics, and music in his cluttered office until the sun rose and bright rays of light filled the room. The office walls are lined with books and patents that he earned during his thirty-year career at the Centers for Disease Control and Prevention (CDC). Such a career was remarkable for a Black man born in 1933 with deep, ebony skin, in a tin roof shack by the muddy train tracks outside of Atlanta, Georgia. His work included evaluating and responding to the medical needs and claims of Macon County, Alabama, residents who were unknowingly exposed to syphilis by the CDC and the United States Public Health Service. Yes, *that* program—the one that we know colloquially as the Tuskegee Experiment. Within the CDC, the program was officially titled the Tuskegee Study of Untreated Syphilis in the Negro Male and was active up until 1972. My granddad is living history in his own right, and he passed a glimmer of his aptitude on to me. So it made complete sense that when I was overcome with emotion and excitement after my interview with Congresswoman Barbara Lee on SiriusXM in February 2022, my granddad was the first person I called.

After appearing on SiriusXM shows across the radio network for about two years as a political analyst, I was granted the opportunity to host an hour-long show as part of their *Pass the Mic* series for newer Black and brown on-air talent. I had full editorial freedom to speak to whomever I wanted about any topic I could dream up. Considering that it was the fiftieth anniversary of Shirley Chisholm's groundbreaking 1972 presidential campaign, I booked one of her longtime mentees, and a key leader of her California campaign team, Congresswoman Barbara Lee. Lee could share an insider's take on the dynamics of the campaign during that time, and I was thrilled when she agreed to the interview. My interview preparations included reading Chisholm's books recounting her congressional run, *Unbought and Unbossed*, and her presidential run, *The Good Fight*; watching Shola Lynch's humanizing documentary, *Chisholm '72*; and watching Congresswoman Lee's documentary, *Speaking Truth to Power.* Armed with context and a human understanding of Shirley Chisholm, I was beyond ready. Or so I thought.

"I was the one who talked to the Black Panther Party, to Huey Newton, to get them involved in voter registration and her campaign,"

Congresswoman Lee said casually. "And I actually... took Huey Newton to a fundraiser at Diahann Carroll's house in Los Angeles so he could meet Shirley Chisholm, and get to know her, so they could get committed to getting involved in the campaign."

At this point in the interview, I let out a combined scream and gasp. *Did she just say what I think she said?* A young Barbara Lee convinced the iconic revolutionary Huey P. Newton to engage in a presidential campaign for the first Black woman to seek the Democratic nomination? And Lee went to the home of *the* Diahann Carroll? The same Diahann Carroll who perfectly portrayed Whitley Gilbert's mother on *A Different World*, opposite Patti LaBelle? The same Diahann Carroll who, thanks to my parents' love of film, I recognized from watching movies like *Claudine*, *Sister, Sister*, and *Eve's Bayou*? The singer, dancer, and actor who commanded every film set or stage she entered? Congresswoman Lee laughed at my delight.

Before I could collect myself, she then added the cherry on top: "...and [Diahann Carroll's house was] where I met Maxine Waters. I think she actually maybe coordinated it..." I could easily imagine a younger version of Representative Maxine Waters in my mind. She must have been in her early thirties in 1972, and just as clear and vibrant a voice as she has been in Congress, including when she effectively "reclaimed her time" during a contentious congressional hearing. For Congresswoman Waters to have potentially been involved in convening such a dynamic group of change makers and cultural icons was mind-boggling. What's more was that I, and many others, had never heard about this tremendous piece of political and cultural history.

After Congresswoman Lee confirmed it all, I asked her if she recognized that she is living, breathing Black history? The congresswoman quipped, "That was just part of my work with Shirley."

This is more than I could have ever wished for in my first time hosting a show on SiriusXM. Slowly, I began to fathom the weight of this historic, and completely un-casual, meetup that took place at the home of a bona fide superstar. This party, mentioned first as an aside, quickly took over our interview time because it was an intentional gathering that brought together historical figures who may not have ever come together under any other circumstances. I understood how special it was to have this entire story on the record—what it could signify for the culture, and how it's all still connected to politics today. I knew I needed to dig deeper into what I learned from Congresswoman Lee. But first, I had to call my granddad.

"Oh, you were among Black *royalty*, baby," he chuckled. I laughed and nodded my head excitedly, even though he couldn't see me. "Shirley Chisholm, Diahann Carroll, Huey Newton—they reminded all of us of what we were capable of as a people," he added. I explained every detail that I had learned in the interview. This party not only brought together political and cultural icons. It also personified how Shirley Chisholm's presidential campaign spoke directly to the role of women, young people, Black people, revolutionaries, and activists as critical components of the health and preservation of the democratic process. She recognized that the people whose communities had been most dismissed could wield their power as a unified collective, and her campaign drew them all in. My granddad, a man of eighty-eight years at the time, understood the rich significance of Shirley Chisholm's campaign in 1972 and this party. We both knew that my interview had unlocked something that needed to be shared.

Today, the historical significance and relevance of Chisholm's presidential campaign and power-building strategy only intensifies as Republicans and white supremacists are hell-bent on erasing Black history and Black people in the United States. As the American democratic institution is threatened and weakened by extremists with each passing election cycle. As women's rights are being taken away, one by one. And as the Democratic Party, which is fueled by women, specifically Black women, still takes their collective power for granted as evidenced by their unwillingness to reciprocate their enthusiastic, unwavering support when they seek public office. The irony is not lost on me, and it wasn't lost on my granddad either.

Riding high on curiosity and sheer adrenaline, I started digging for more details about the party. I just couldn't leave it there. I was desperate to learn more about this fundraiser, who else attended, and how it impacted Chisholm's campaign. As my interview with Congresswoman Lee replayed on a loop in my mind, I began probing memoirs, archived interviews, files from the Federal Bureau of Investigation, and newspapers from the time.

My research confirmed that on April 29, 1972, five weeks before the California Democratic Primary election, a magical party unfolded in Beverly Hills. Diahann Carroll welcomed Shirley Chisholm to Southern California, and she heralded the private event in the press, lending her name and her celebrity to the campaign. The guest list that I managed to piece together was full of surprises: Flip Wilson paused his comedy tour to participate, Huey P. Newton and Barbara Lee were surveilled by federal and state law enforcement every step of the way to the soiree, and Goldie Hawn drifted through the event without a date—which was apparently scandalous at the time. In one photo of the party, Berry Gordy is seen hugging Diahann Carroll as British journalist David Frost spoke to other guests in the background. These were icons of the era, lasting figures in American pop culture who somehow, from all corners of their respective industries, ended up in the same room together for one person. Every attendee that I confirmed was there played a clear role in the democratic experiment that Chisholm was conducting, and they mirrored the multiracial, multigenerational coalition that she was building.

Ultimately, after this preliminary round of research, I knew I needed to go back to the source: Congresswoman Lee. Thankfully she obliged.

"You're the first person to ever ask for a follow-up interview about this." I balked in disbelief. Why hadn't anyone probed deeper into this party?

Yes, many people know that Shirley Chisholm was the first Black woman to serve in Congress and to run for the Democratic nomination for president. Many are familiar with her famous saying, "If they don't give you a seat at the table, bring a folding chair," an analogy for daring to take up space. But she was so much more than that. Shirley Chisholm was the daughter of immigrants who cut her own path. She was a poet, a pianist, a dancer, and a designer. She was an activist leader. She was the dynamic woman who could command a party full of celebrities at Diahann Carroll's mansion with ease and verve. And by uncovering her layers and heeding her clear vision, we can learn timeless lessons about power—building it and leveraging it, even in today's fraught political reality.

As I was researching this project, I found myself repeatedly mumbling, "Shirley Chisholm called it." She knew that in order to restore power to the people, and to give Black and brown candidates and women candidates a shot at winning elections, special interest money had no place in politics. She knew that the only way to gain political power was to unite people across every demographic identity—expanding the tent that the Democratic Party has attempted to build. She knew that the media had to record and transmit her humanity to the masses, just as much as they highlighted their negative feelings about her existence in their coverage, if they chose to cover her at all.

And she knew that rejecting rules, norms, and traditions was the only way to shift entire systems for the people.

The history that I was learning extended beyond the reductive view of Shirley Chisholm as "the first," or a symbolic figure that many have come to know. This history emphasized Chisholm's legacy and contextualized it in the power of organizing and being in community with others as a pathway toward our collective well-being. This party was so much more than a get-together with famous people sipping champagne. It was an intentional moment that redefined power building in American politics, and each person in attendance played a specific role.

I first began outlining a book to honor Shirley Chisholm's legacy in 2021, and I finished the manuscript in the summer of 2024. Throughout my research and writing process, I arrived at unexpected realizations and conclusions about how Shirley Chisholm's life and legacy can guide us through our fragile society today. And as you step into Diahann Carroll's 1972 mansion, my hope is that you see Chisholm as more than a symbolic figure, but as a human, visionary leader who was perpetually ahead of her time.

CHAPTER ONE

THE PARTY

"As Black women, we have a right and responsibility to define ourselves, and seek our allies in common cause."

—Audre Lorde, *Sister Outsider*

Diahann Carroll knew how to throw a party. The award-winning actress, singer, and Broadway performer had been hosting upscale affairs on both coasts and abroad for years, as her various film productions, performances, and love interests propelled her jet-setting lifestyle and elegant tastes. In preparation for her events, Carroll added her personal flair and finesse to each detail as she'd mastered the art of ensuring that her guests felt welcomed and were treated exquisitely. Even on a normal day in her life, Carroll's home was bustling with at least nine staff and workers, including chauffeurs, cooks, gardeners, and a nanny for her daughter, Suzanne. On the cool evening of April 29, 1972, Carroll's stream of staff was on hand to valet the guests' cars, keep their glasses filled with libations, and usher them into the throng of supporters and curious attendees. Carroll's estate was bursting with celebrity, exuberance, and history in support of the first Black person, and the first woman, to seek the Democratic nomination for president. The Welcome to Hollywood party for the Honorable Shirley Chisholm, US Representative of New York, was kicking into high gear.

Vibrant chatter and a smooth bass line wafted through the soft spring breeze as cultural icons, revolutionaries, and Hollywood power players cascaded toward the cobblestone entrance of Carroll's Beverly Hills mansion. As she welcomed the guests into her home alongside her co-host, comedian Flip Wilson, a congregation effortlessly formed in the landscaped backyard. "Exquisite" would be an understatement, as Carroll's private lawn was the equivalent of a lush sanctuary full of citrus trees and rich, tropical greenery. Guests took in every inch of the stunning slate-covered terrace, mingling around the fire pit and enjoying the view of the hills below. Carroll's heated, black-tiled swimming pool gave the illusion of a placid, bottomless fjord under the night sky, the entire oasis accented by a full waterfall feature cascading down thick rocks. Imagining the wide eyes of the guests, who were undoubtedly comparing Carroll's sprawling Beverly Hills estate to their own homes, is almost delightful knowing that Carroll, in partnership with designer Barnett Lewis, took her time to meticulously design her abode with color and warmth. The opulence of it all was almost too much to take in.

Inside, Carroll's home was designed with equal parts comfort and elegance, so that visitors felt relaxed but also knew to be extremely careful not to disturb any of the finery. The vaulted, wood-beamed ceilings and the vibrant, plush lounge sofas made the space feel wide open as guests moved through Carroll's personal retreat. The intricately carved wood and cobblestone details around the fireplaces, which appeared in nearly every room, created a seamless flow that mirrored the front entrance. Carroll's home also featured a floor-to-ceiling wine cellar, an elevator, a billiard room, and a sauna.

The Benedict Canyon home had been built decades earlier by one of the wealthiest women in the world at the time, Woolworth convenience store heiress Barbara Woolworth Hutton, as a birthday gift for her twenty-one-year-old son. A former Woolworth-owned estate was certainly an ironic setting for this historic event for a Black political leader. The nickel and dime store had a firm and well-documented commitment to segregation in the Southern states, and they maintained a staunch adherence to Jim Crow laws across the many stores and restaurants that they owned and operated. Their stores were the precursor to today's dollar stores, and featured lunch counters that only served white customers.

In 1960, four North Carolina Agricultural and Technical College freshmen—Joseph McNeil, Franklin McCain, Ezell Blair Jr., and David Richmond—staged a sit-in at the lunch counter inside the Greensboro Woolworth after being refused service. Their peaceful protest went down in history as the Greensboro sit-in, which then sparked a string of sit-ins nationwide that led to the Woolworth store's desegregation and inspired the founding of the Student Nonviolent Coordinating Committee (SNCC). So while our evening's hostess wrapped every guest in a luxurious, welcoming embrace, it's safe to assume that Barbara Woolworth Hutton's family, who was still expanding the Woolworth franchise in the early 1970s, would have clutched their pearls at the sight of such an occasion hosted by two Black superstars, for a Black guest of honor, and with a multicultural audience.

After all, this is *the* Diahann Carroll we're talking about, the triple threat who first made her name as a singer touring jazz clubs and appearing on primetime television shows like *The Ed Sullivan Show*. She's the entertainment icon whom we remember today for her starring role as Dominique Deveraux in *Dynasty*, who Carroll personally dubbed the first ever "rich, Black bitch" on television. She demanded that the show producers develop Deveraux's storyline as though she were a "white man who wanted to be wealthy and powerful" as a direct challenge to any limitations that producers, or viewers for that matter, had in mind to place on her character. At that time, Black characters and women on television were shifting from stereotypical roles that lacked substance and nuance into well-rounded characters who challenged their white and male co-stars to drive storylines forward. As Carroll was the first Black lead to appear on *Dynasty*, she embodied this new standard from the moment she debuted on-screen wearing a cream suit and flawless makeup, and issuing demands with her first lines. In a very different role, Carroll portrayed the complex and distinctly human struggle of a single mother of six children in the film *Claudine*, which garnered her an Oscar nomination for best actress. She also starred as the titular character in *Julia*, a weekly

NBC sitcom where she played a widowed nurse and mother navigating a middle-class lifestyle and career. *Julia* was the first primetime network sitcom starring a Black woman, and was nothing short of groundbreaking. This performance earned her an Emmy nomination and a Golden Globe Award for best actress. *Julia* also expanded Carroll's fan base to families and children who would seek her out for autographs—a stark departure from her experiences interacting with fans as a performer at upscale lounges and nightclubs.

As rewarding as working on *Julia* was, the experience drained Carroll physically, mentally, and emotionally. The weekly filming schedule proved so grueling that Carroll spent time in and out of the hospital battling exhaustion and lingering illness throughout production. Carroll had been running her career at breakneck speed, juggling her singing performances, Broadway shows, and family commitments. After three seasons, she couldn't take it anymore. She opted to walk away from the series, and the show came to an abrupt end in 1971. The choice was bittersweet for Carroll, because *Julia* elevated her career and expanded how Black people were portrayed on-screen; however, given her health concerns, she decided to prioritize her own survival.

After exiting her hit television show, Carroll took up the political charge of supporting Shirley Chisholm's presidential campaign. She knew what it meant to be a Black woman driving substantive, positive change that resisted social norms and stereotypes. From portraying relatable, endearing characters to demanding that scripts reject conventional boundaries, Carroll presented new layers of nuance, on- and off-screen, that challenged audiences and producers to see and respect Black women.

Having carved through the steel of discrimination and structural limitations in the entertainment industry, Carroll saw clear parallels between her career and Chisholm's political goals.

Authenticity was Shirley Chisholm's trademark. She was intent on resetting social and political expectations, and forcing people to confront their own biases by showing up as exactly who she was in all spaces—be that in the streets of Brooklyn, the halls of Congress, or televised interviews. It's something that she had been doing for her entire life. As the eldest daughter of immigrants from Barbados and Guyana, Chisholm, then Shirley Anita St. Hill, was born in Brooklyn, New York, where she lived until she was three. She then spent the next six years of her childhood on a lush farm in Barbados with her two sisters, her maternal grandmother, an aunt, an uncle, and a gaggle of cousins. Each morning, she collected water from the well, carefully balancing the bucket between her tiny arms. Her daily routine also included feeding and caring for the goats, pigs, chickens, and other animals, and attending school in a one-room schoolhouse that served 125 students. Her childhood on the island left a deep mark on her character, as she learned that education and discipline were pathways to achieving her dreams, and that her Blackness was a source of pride. These were the roots of her unshakable confidence in her skills, and her fearlessness about speaking up and challenging "age old traditions," which later defined her career.

Returning to America in 1934 at nine years old was a jolt to young Shirley's system. The Great Depression was raging, her family was receiving public assistance to survive, and her American teachers did not recognize her academic aptitude. At school, she withstood the mean taunts of children who mocked her ill-fitting, state-issued clothing, which hung off her thin, wire-framed body. She also began to act out due to her boredom. Placed in a classroom with children two years younger than she, Shirley would quickly finish her lessons and then fire spitballs when her teacher wasn't looking. Once the school recognized and satiated her advanced academic abilities with additional instruction, she excelled. Her spunk and fearlessness also translated into her professional work years later when she became a teacher after graduating from Brooklyn College in 1946.

With the end of World War II, Chisholm had to compete for a teaching job against the influx of more experienced educators who had served in the war and were returning to their old positions. She also had to compete against school administrators' skeptical reactions to her petite, ninety-pound stature and youthful face as they repeatedly turned her away for looking too young. She was twenty-two years old. Chisholm ultimately secured a position after several rounds of interviewing and losing her temper with the director of the Mt. Calvary Child Care Center in Harlem. Sensing that another rejection was on the way, she declared, "Give me a chance to show you!" Chisholm certainly showed her, using her musical and creative gifts to engage her classroom full of four-year-olds with dancing, singing, and piano playing.

That tenacity and perseverance fueled Chisholm's early experiences in politics as she smashed through sexist barriers that were reinforced by political leaders and voters in Brooklyn. As a volunteer with local Brooklyn Democratic clubs, she spent years maneuvering behind the scenes, fundraising and printing materials to share in the community, until she essentially dared her club to pass her over for a vacant seat in the state assembly because she "wear[s] a skirt." When she successfully ran for the New York State Assembly in 1964 and then Congress in 1968, opponents and voters attempted to diminish her skills and leadership abilities by telling her that she "ought to be home..." cooking for her husband, and referring to her as a "little school teacher." Chisholm responded by winning both elections the best way she knew how—by leaning on her intimate ties to the Bedford-Stuyvesant neighborhood and her decade of activism with local organizations to rally women voters across her home turf.

While some may be familiar with Chisholm's famous quote, "If they don't give you a seat at the table, then bring a folding chair," that notion captures only half of her ethos. The other half was demonstrated in her unwavering commitment to upending a political system that neglected and ignored the people and their needs. As a congresswoman, Chisholm stayed ahead of the curve. She jump-started her first term with legislative proposals that would effectively flip the table altogether.

Chisholm sponsored legislation to establish a basic family income, advance racial and gender equity, and abolish the military draft during the Vietnam War. Her policy proposals didn't stop at the big headline items either. Chisholm was sure to address the fundamental components undergirding these broader issues, as seen in her proposal for a basic family income. In 1969, 24.3 million people in America were living below the poverty line, and Black people, and other people of color, "constituted 31 percent of the poor... although they collectively comprised 12 percent of the total population." Given her intimate understanding of poverty, and having received public assistance as a child in Brooklyn during the Depression, Chisholm proposed legislation that would provide a comprehensive response to people's needs. She buttressed a proposal for a basic income of $6,500 for a family of four with proposals for a commission dedicated to consumer protections, the creation of a national network of childcare centers, and tax code modifications that would expand benefits for unmarried people, particularly single parents. She proposed changing entire family care systems to deliver on the real-time needs of her constituents, which would in turn increase equity and access for people from a whole host of backgrounds. What's striking is that these are policy proposals that political candidates continue to campaign with today. And as further testament of being well ahead of her time, Chisholm's efforts, had they been heeded, could have saved the nation from the family care crisis we're witnessing today. At present, nearly 6.5 million families struggle to find childcare, and businesses lose $12.7 billion annually as their employees experience childcare issues.

In addition to her proposals to address poverty and childcare needs, Chisholm's firm opposition to the Vietnam War was also attractive to a broad swath of voters. In Congress, Chisholm not only proposed legislation to end the draft, but also protested the war by voting against every Defense funding bill that was brought to the House floor, a commitment she made during her inaugural floor speech. She also rejected bills authorizing the use of antiballistic missiles, and advanced proposals for more jobs and benefits for veterans.

Chisholm's foresight and her commitment to changing systems in service of all of the American people were central to her work as a congresswoman and served as the crux of her 1972 presidential campaign platform. She was ahead of the Democratic Party leadership at the time, who rarely backed up her proposals and often stated publicly that she had gone too far. And as they failed to buy into Chisholm's groundbreaking proposals, voters across demographics saw an appeal in Chisholm's efforts, and they flocked to her coalition of support. Her comprehensive approach demonstrated to veterans, students, Black people, Latino people, Asian people, people living with disabilities, and people living in poverty that her ideas and her actions could grant them a better way of living. They saw change that could flip political and policy priorities in their favor, and they were drawn to its source.

Without a doubt, it was these ideas and actions that drew Diahann Carroll to Shirley Chisholm. In a quote to the *LA Times*, Carroll noted, "She's got some ideas that can turn this country around." That's why Carroll went above and beyond to show her support for Chisholm publicly. Carroll performed at rallies for Chisholm's campaign in New York. She sang Chisholm's praises to the press. And she opened her home in April 1972 and hosted the only fundraising cocktail party for Chisholm's campaign in Los Angeles. While supporting political efforts wasn't necessarily new for Carroll, it was extremely rare for her to personally host political fêtes at her home. In fact, noted Carroll, the only other remotely political event that she hosted at her home was for the Student Nonviolent Coordinating Committee, yet another irony considering that the birth of SNCC was due to Woolworth stores' racist policies.

Despite Carroll's early support of Chisholm, her decision to host the Welcome to Hollywood party was surprising news for Chisholm's California campaign team. While they were unclear about precisely why Carroll granted them the honor, they were thrilled by her continued support of the campaign and her willingness to provide Chisholm access to her Hollywood network. Immediately upon announcing her presidential campaign in January 1972, Chisholm joined the Democratic presidential primary sprint alongside thirteen other candidates. Each candidate sought to win state primary elections ahead of the Democratic National Convention. They all had their eye on the Democratic presidential nomination as they traveled across the nation, making their pitches to Democratic voters about why they were the best representative of the Democratic Party, their vision for the future of the nation, and in turn, their fitness to lead the nation. By April 1972, Chisholm's California campaign team was just beginning to find a rhythm. Most of the state's team were unpaid volunteers or on loan from national political groups like Chisholm's California campaign coordinator, Arlie Scott. Scott joined the campaign that month after transitioning from her role as the director of the National Organization for Women's Center for Women's Studies in Los Angeles. And California was a tricky primary state because it was one of the last "winner-take-all" Democratic primaries in the nation in 1972, meaning the distribution of delegates among the fourteen candidates on the ballot was not proportionate to the number of votes they received. Instead, the state's Democratic Party rules dictated that the candidate who won the most primary votes would win all of the 271 California delegates. As a result, no matter how many voters supported Chisholm in the California Democratic primary, their preference would ultimately be ignored.

Winning California wasn't ever a possibility for Chisholm. When measured against her opponents, she had a financial deficit, a name recognition deficit, a campaign infrastructure deficit, and an advertising deficit. And yet earning a strong show of support from California voters remained important to demonstrating broad support for her campaign and showing publicly that she was capable of building a coalition that could issue demands during policy negotiations for the official Democratic Party platform. Winning wasn't Chisholm's goal; power building was.

The Welcome to Hollywood party, timed just five weeks before the California primary election, was poised to provide a boost in visibility that could begin to address some of Chisholm's comparatively low campaign funds. Closing that gap meant more resources to print flyers, run ads in newspapers, buy campaign literature to hand to voters while volunteers canvassed communities, and spread the word about Chisholm's vision for the people and for the nation before the early June primary election.

The stakes were high, and Diahann Carroll called in her network to help power Chisholm's campaign. Throughout the evening, cultural influencers such as Motown Records founder and musical executive Berry Gordy, revolutionary Black Panther Party co-founder Huey P. Newton, Oscar-winning actress Goldie Hawn, and British journalist David Frost flowed into Carroll's mansion to meet the presidential candidate and socialize among the stars. Carroll leveraged her social capital to create an audience of heavy hitters for Chisholm, and Chisholm had them all enthralled as only she could. She knew that by engaging these figures with Carroll's support, her reach could expand to their fans across music, film, television, and media.

Shirley Chisholm knew how to shine in this crowd by doing exactly what she always did: being her charming, witty, candid self. It's easy to imagine her and Diahann Carroll laughing together, Chisholm sharing stories about confronting men in Congress, and Carroll matching her with tales of how she did the same on the set of *Julia*. One can also picture Chisholm greeting each starlet, activist, and Hollywood executive with a warmth and resolve that communicated her humanity, her empathy, and her fortitude. As guests gathered around the black tile pool, the crowd would have easily loomed over Chisholm, who stood at five foot three, as they leaned in closely to hear her every word, and she would not have been the least bit unnerved by it. She was used to attracting and engaging with large groups of people—the antithesis of those politicians who would rather hide out in a quiet back room waiting for a crowd to assemble before delivering a speech or filtering through questions. Rather, Chisholm moved through the crowd at Diahann Carroll's home with the same confidence and comfort that she had when she walked the halls of Congress.

She was especially masterful at leaving her mark during individual conversations. Person by person, Chisholm outlined her vision and her platform that prioritized action for the American people. Ever consistent, it was precisely the same message that she delivered on college campuses, in interviews with the press, and with workers across the nation. Shirley Chisholm didn't shift her tone just because she was in Hollywood. If anything, she doubled down on her forthright mannerisms in front of this crowd. The *Southwest News* captured her declaration to the fundraiser guests that "some 'soul' was needed in the White House, and [she] urged all minorities... and young people to unite to 'put it together.'" Chisholm's plea for action and unity struck a chord that reverberated across the crowd of leaders, icons, and stars. She understood that each person at the party—the activists, the political donors, the young people, the media mavens, the feminists, and others—each represented a key ingredient of her power-building efforts. With every conversation, as champagne glasses clinked in the background, Chisholm was strengthening her coalition.

CHAPTER TWO

THE MONEY

"Cash rules everything around me."

—Wu-Tang Clan, "C.R.E.A.M."

Shirley Chisholm received her biggest California campaign donation the night of the Welcome to Hollywood party. Up to that point, this particular donor had never publicly supported a political candidate. But now, at the height of his career, he was prepared to break his biggest rule in a big way for Chisholm. Plus, it made sense that Flip Wilson, one of the brightest stars at Diahann Carroll's home that night, would also serve as co-host of the fundraiser.

Wherever Wilson went, he knew how to make it a party, and in 1972, he was on fire. The comedian was the hottest name in entertainment with the most in-demand show on television. *The Flip Wilson Show* on NBC brought in 40 million viewers week after week. Given its popularity, NBC increased the advertiser's fee to $86,000 per minute. And *Time* magazine dubbed Wilson "TV's First Black Superstar" in a cover story that January.

The Emmy, Grammy, Peabody, and Golden Globe Award–winning comedian, host, and performer had come a long way from Jersey City, New Jersey. As the tenth of two dozen children born to his parents, the concept of home eluded Wilson after his mother abandoned the family and emptied his father's bank account. Wilson bounced around foster homes and reform school before enlisting in the Air Force at sixteen years old. After surviving four years of service and a deployment to Guam during the Korean War, Wilson tackled his comedy career with a deep determination, and desperation, for success. In a matter of fifteen years, Wilson went from sleeping in pay toilets and performing on the Chitlin' Circuit (Black-owned dive bars and venues throughout the South and the Midwest) to successfully negotiating to retain the syndication rights to his eponymous network show.

Wilson was intentional about featuring the biggest entertainers, athletes, and stars of the moment on his show, from The Supremes and Johnny Cash to Muhammad Ali and Bill Russell. Wilson also routinely featured his beloved drag character "Geraldine Jones" on his prime-time comedy show. "Geraldine" was named after a young girl in Wilson's elementary school class whom he had a crush on, and the character's mannerisms were modeled after the Southern Black women Wilson observed in the front rows of his shows while on the Chitlin' Circuit. Wilson summarized the character's top qualities: "she's honest, she's frank, she's affectionate, she's independent," and when she was onstage, she stole the show. In a 1971 sketch during the first season of *The Flip Wilson Show*, "Geraldine" swiveled in her chair playfully next to renowned British journalist David Frost in a purple Emilio Pucci shift dress, matching purple tights and shoes, thick false lashes, and a $450 wig. Ever faithful to her boyfriend, Killer, she rejected each of Frost's friendly gestures. When Frost attempted to kiss her hand while greeting her, "Geraldine" quickly snatched it away saying, "Watch what you kiss, honey." The crowd roared. After Frost offered her a cigarette, "Geraldine" quipped, "I don't drink, I don't smoke, and I don't do windows." Frost could barely contain his laughter during the sketch, which ended with him scooping up "Geraldine" into his arms and carrying her off the orange-carpeted stage where Flip's name was spelled in lights.

While millions of viewers loved "Geraldine," some considered the character to be "an insult to black womanhood" because of how crudely she behaved. Others considered the sketch emasculating because Wilson was performing in drag. Wilson repeatedly rejected the criticisms saying that "Geraldine's liberated—that's where she's at. Everybody knows she don't take no stuff." That was part of the character's appeal to Shirley Chisholm. Chisholm particularly appreciated "Geraldine's" catchphrase, "What you see is what you get," because it matched her own tone and approach to politics. There was no fluff, no platitudes, no beating around the bush when Chisholm advocated for the people. There was only a straight-talking, passionate leader with undeniable clarity about her mission. That parallel to "Geraldine" was certainly appealing to someone like Flip Wilson. So appealing that he was willing to publicly declare his support for Chisholm's presidential campaign, an explicit break from his long-standing rule not to engage in politics.

To Wilson, politics were a far stretch from comedic life. As he told the press through the years, "... the difference between comics and politicians is that in comedy you sound as though you're serious and they know it's a joke, but in politics they expect you to be serious and you sound like you're joking. I don't like politics because I like the truth." Needless to say, politicians were not featured on his variety show. Still, there were guests and sketches that made political statements. Muhammad Ali appeared as a guest in January 1971, four years after he was convicted of draft evasion during the Vietnam War, and months before his Supreme Court case on the matter was decided. Wilson's opinions about the war, the Black liberation movement, and other pressing matters in 1970s America served as an undercurrent on his show, as he viewed himself as a champion of the truth who also prioritized mass appeal. He surely saw those same values within Shirley Chisholm and her presidential campaign, at least to the degree that he'd grant an exception to his practice of keeping politics and politicians at arm's length. It also helped that Diahann Carroll's ex-husband, Monte Kay, was Flip Wilson's longtime manager. It was likely a quick call from Kay that probably sealed Wilson's role as a co-host for the Welcome to Hollywood fundraiser. This is Hollywood after all, folks!

When Shirley Chisholm decided to run for the Democratic nomination for the presidency, she made one thing clear: local donations and grassroots fundraising would be the lifeblood of her campaign. She was "unbought and unbossed," and thus not beholden to anyone but the people whom she endeavored to serve. As soon as she made her official campaign announcement in January 1972, Chisholm's earliest, most ardent supporters—young people and women in particular—raised donations on their own and sent them to Chisholm's Washington, DC, and Brooklyn offices. Envelopes with five- and ten-dollar bills arrived in flurries and were an early signal of the public's direct interest and support for her historic campaign.

Between January and April 1972, Chisholm's California team hosted small community events, tea parties, and rallies where the campaign gratefully collected anything people could offer. Similar to the envelopes of dollar bills Chisholm received, her supporters in the state gave the change from their pockets to show their support. They contributed to the campaign because they believed in her policy ideas to address poverty, provide childcare, and end the Vietnam War. To them, Chisholm's policies were responsive to their needs, a change from the way other elected officials had neglected their communities. And while their donations did not deliver sizable, sustainable financial support, they did represent hope for Chisholm and hope for their collective future.

Chisholm knew that running for president would be expensive, and that if people were sending her dollars and cents from their own pockets, she wanted to use their resources wisely. Thus, those early small-dollar donations doubled as a critical planning tool: an indicator for where Chisholm's campaign would invest time, energy, and resources, and where she had the best opportunity to win delegates. Each envelope that contained a campaign donation or a letter of support was like a data point on a map of the United States. Within each data point, voters were confirming how much they supported Shirley

Chisholm's platform, how they were organizing their community or their campus, and how ready they were to vote for her to become the Democratic nominee for president. These data points were hot spots for fundraising, a critical ingredient for the campaign. So when people in Florida, North Carolina, Massachusetts, New York, New Jersey, California, and Michigan declared that they were forming local organizing and resource hubs for Chisholm, those states became electoral priorities for the campaign because they were already ripe for engagement.

The California team was dealt a lucky hand when Diahann Carroll offered to throw a bash for Shirley Chisholm at her home to properly introduce her to leaders in the entertainment industry. During the fundraiser, Flip Wilson was so moved and impressed by Chisholm's call to action in her speech that he handed her campaign staff a check for $5,000. Chisholm's team was bowled over. Arlie Scott, the state campaign coordinator, described her shock: "I don't think we had any idea after getting buckets of money here and there and getting little bits and trying to put things on the back of paper, for Flip Wilson to hand us a check for $5,000, it was just like (gasps)..." That was more money than the campaign had ever received from one supporter. According to campaign finance reports, it was roughly 18 percent of Chisholm's campaign budget in California that quarter. And while it may be a reflex to scoff at that amount, that $5,000 check written in 1972 is worth about $40,000 today. It was a considerable donation, and for Chisholm's team, it felt utterly massive. Scott was rightfully overwhelmed.

Wu-Tang Clan got it right. Cash does indeed rule everything around us. While the seminal rappers used the classic track "C.R.E.A.M." to describe the struggle to get cash in order to survive in the streets, that same reality translates to politics, where money also represents power and possibility. Cash injections into political campaigns yield higher voter engagement, higher message amplification, and a higher probability of electoral success. Chisholm experienced that financial struggle while fighting to break through during the Democratic presidential primary. Facing such a steep cash disadvantage, Chisholm's fundraising haul was eclipsed by that of her competitors, who essentially had access to bottomless pits of cash. As a result, Chisholm's opponents had the ad buys, the media placements, the jets, and the bus caravans to travel across the nation, while her campaign lacked these flashy, yet integral resources. Instead of ad buys, she had leaflets that local organizers copied and reprinted. Instead of media placements, she had to sue for equal airtime on television. Instead of a jet to crisscross the nation, she took commercial flights, buses, and car rides from volunteers to reach voters who were often unaware of her presidential campaign until she was able to physically visit their states.

Even before cash influences the expanse of a candidate's campaign, it dictates who can access politics and political office in the first place. As Chisholm wrote in her 1973 book, *The Good Fight*, "Everywhere in this country, there are men and women who have real ability and new solutions to offer, but they will never have a chance to serve in public office because they do not have the money to run and win." The United States' political system is pay-to-play, so these potential leaders are hindered by a lack of financial resources before they even begin to dream or share their big ideas. Ultimately, these untapped leaders do not go far, or their ideas completely wither on the vine, while people who have no business in elected leadership roles (read: Donald Trump) seemingly pay their way into political prominence. And because of that access to money, or even the perception of having wealth, these rogue leaders emerge and do their damnedest to destroy our most basic institutions, which were already historically fragmented and exclusive. And yes, that includes our democracy itself. In the case of Trump, his acts resulted in 91 criminal, felony charges at the federal and state levels, a criminal conviction on 34 counts in New York, attempting to overturn the will of the voters during the 2020 election with calls to state and local election workers, and lighting the fire for an armed mob to attack the US Capitol on January 6, 2021.

Chisholm understood that the most direct way to decrease the influence of money in elections and to increase voters' power was through removing all private money from politics. In her trademark posture of upending inefficient and inequitable systems, Chisholm believed that money from special interest groups, and money from a candidate's personal store of wealth, should be banned. This would level the field, and people who are not individually wealthy would have a viable shot at undercutting wealthy candidates' ability to simply write themselves a check or disproportionately cater to wealthy donors and corporations who finance their campaigns. Instead, shorter, publicly funded elections would center voters and their needs. And candidates would be required to address as much of the public as possible and propose expansive, substantive platforms in order to compete for votes. Chisholm's goals were to put the people first, and to improve how democracy functions. To demonstrate her commitment, Chisholm banned special interest money from her own campaign, and reached out to as many voters as possible across the nation. She ran her campaign as close to this ideal as possible, and when she did accept donations from wealthy individuals, like Flip Wilson, she ensured that their political goals aligned with her campaign. That intentional discernment facilitated a mutual respect, and a principled campaign.

Chisholm enjoyed support from heavy hitters and everyday people, but it wasn't all support for Chisholm when she announced her presidential campaign. Just before her official campaign launch on January 25, 1972, national political leaders and operatives signaled that they were put off by Chisholm's candidacy, proactively claiming "widespread dissatisfaction" with the congresswoman. In Brooklyn, the head of Operation Breadbasket, a nonprofit committed to promoting the economic interests of Black people, convened press on the eve of her campaign announcement to posit, "What has she done," and "I see no appreciable changes." Chisholm also recounted to the *New York Times* how Mayor John V. Lindsay of New York told her on Christmas Eve in 1971 that she would cut into his vote if she ran for president. Chisholm replied, "That's the same thing McGovern told me...but goddammit, this is the American Dream—the chance for a Black woman to run for the highest office. If you're so worried about cutting into the progressive vote, why don't you and McGovern get together—and one of you decide to back out?"

Senator George McGovern, a two-term senator from South Dakota, was making his second run for the Democratic nomination in 1972. While there was some alignment among the broad areas of interest in his and Chisholm's platforms, including the Vietnam War and responding to rampant poverty, McGovern's policy approach lacked urgency, and his actions often ran counter to his promises. Like Chisholm, McGovern opposed the Vietnam War in 1972, but unlike Chisholm, he had approved millions of dollars in military appropriations throughout the nearly twenty-year war. Like Chisholm, McGovern supported withdrawing US troops from Southeast Asia, and he co-sponsored the McGovern-Hatfield Amendment to set a deadline for withdrawal, but unlike Chisholm, he placed conditions on the withdrawal and offered President Nixon loopholes instead of calling for the immediate return of all US service members in the region. McGovern also supported a minimum income for families, but unlike Chisholm, he wouldn't commit to a plan to realize this policy goal as a member of Congress, though he claimed he would outline a plan if elected president. The intention to improve people's lives was there. The money most certainly was there. But the follow-through and execution were absent.

Within the Democratic Party, attempting to exclude Chisholm from the political dialogue of the moment was sensitive ground to tread. Democrats didn't want to upset Black voters by publicly dismissing Chisholm—though some Black elected officials worked to undermine her candidacy all by themselves. At the same time, Democrats saw Chisholm as a threat who could take critical votes away from McGovern in the primary, and a threat to their own political endeavors in the future, as New York Mayor Lindsay reportedly expressed. Either way, a target was on Chisholm's back because the party had no idea how to engage a candidate who was a woman, a Black person, a daughter of immigrants, and absolutely resolute in her convictions. Ultimately, they feared the unknown.

The reality that money and resources were scarce, and support among political leaders was limited, did not deter Chisholm. If anything, the lack of resources prompted her to ramp up her scrappy nature, which was established during her childhood in Barbados, before returning to New York during the Depression. In 1968, Chisholm tapped into her tenacity when she won her congressional seat against a candidate with abundant resources, thanks in large part to "personal contact and sustained effort," combined with her direct connection to the community. She would ride through the Brooklyn streets with a caravan of cars covered in Chisholm signs and speak to voters from a megaphone. She would greet voters on street corners and in housing projects, and ask for their support. Even when supporters attempted to host fundraisers and house parties for her, Chisholm would help to provide money for tea and refreshments. She understood that campaigning and fundraising are contact sports, and that time spent in-person with voters and supporters could not be replaced. She also knew how to stretch every fundraised dollar, including that $5,000 contribution from Flip Wilson during her presidential campaign.

Wilson's donation was the rocket fuel desperately needed to finance efforts to mobilize voters across forty-three congressional districts in California. With it, Chisholm could buy ad space in newspapers and radio stations, print campaign brochures and materials, and expand awareness and support for her historic candidacy. That organizing led to Chisholm winning nearly 5 percent of the vote (more than 138,000 votes) in the California Democratic primary in June 1972, a feat that demonstrated yet again that Chisholm's campaign was punching above its weight. In the weeks before the primary, polling data showed Chisholm, the first Black person to ever run in the presidential primary, with well below 2 percent of support among California voters.

With Flip Wilson's contribution alone, the Welcome to Hollywood party was one of the Chisholm campaign's most successful events. The star-studded evening built on previous, smaller fundraisers on the East Coast hosted by Black celebrities eager to lend their names and their talents to amplify Chisholm's candidacy. Back in New York, on Chisholm's home turf, there had been a rotation of activities organized and attended by artists and actors from Harry Belafonte and Ruby Dee to Sidney Poitier and Richard Roundtree. "*Black royalty*," as my grandfather would describe them.

In February 1972, Harry and Julie Belafonte opened their home to the Chisholm campaign for a small gathering. A few weeks prior to the Beverly Hills fundraiser, Diahann Carroll, Ossie Davis, Lena Horne, Roberta Flack, and others hosted a benefit concert at the

Palace Theatre in New York City that made waves in local news and garnered support for the campaign.

To put that into perspective, these individuals were multi-talented legends in the entertainment industry. Harry Belafonte was a triple threat, an Emmy-winning actor and performer who made audiences swoon with his Caribbean-inspired music and striking smile. Belafonte supplemented his passion for the arts with activism and engagement in the civil rights movement. To have the biggest names in music, television, theater, and Black culture embrace and celebrate Chisholm at a moment when she was being publicly rejected by the Democratic Party and Black political leaders was invaluable. Invaluable not only to her campaign's ability to continue voter outreach, but also to boost the campaign's morale during the primary election season.

Still, even with support from some of the brightest Black stars and performers of the time, Shirley Chisholm managed to raise only a fraction of the millions of dollars that the eventual Democratic nominee, Senator George McGovern, ultimately spent to win the presidential primary. Unfortunately, too few voters considered Shirley Chisholm to be a leader worthy of their donations. The proof is in the numbers. During the 1972 Democratic primary, Senator McGovern raised and spent $12 million, Senator Edmund Muskie raised and spent $7 million, and Senator Hubert Humphrey raised and spent $4.7 million. Meanwhile, Chisholm spent roughly $300,000 for the entirety of the campaign. When adjusted for inflation, the gap is overwhelmingly stark at Chisholm's $2.25 million compared to McGovern's nearly $1 billion. That fundraising disparity hasn't shifted much for Black women in politics since 1972.

Now, before you shout that the United States has had a Black and South Asian woman serve as vice president, recall that Vice

President Kamala Harris was dogged by repeated questions about electability in the 2020 Democratic presidential primary election, nearly fifty years after Shirley Chisholm faced those same questions. For example, in May 2019, four months into her own presidential campaign, reporters swarmed then-Senator Harris after a town hall event in New Hampshire to ask if she would consider being Joe Biden's vice presidential candidate. The notion was absurd at the time, as the race had only just begun. The media and leading voices in politics preemptively deemed Harris to be an unelectable presidential candidate before Democratic primary voters had an opportunity to cast a single ballot. In the moment, Harris used humor to respond saying, "I think that Joe Biden would be a great running mate. As vice president, he's proven that he knows how to do the job." While she pivoted confidently and appropriately, the narrative was already set, and even supported by the Congressional Black Caucus, who called a Biden-Harris ticket a "dream ticket."

Poll after poll showed how voters doubted her skills and abilities, despite her record of service spanning decades prior. Harris lagged behind her Democratic primary competitors in the fundraising push, too. Senator Bernie Sanders hauled in $109 million, Senator Elizabeth Warren raised $82 million, then-Mayor Pete Buttigieg raised $77 million, and Joe Biden raised $61 million by the end of 2019. Joe Biden went on to raise more than $1 billion by the end of the 2020 Democratic primary election, which surely helped him win the presidency. When Kamala Harris suspended her presidential campaign in December 2019, she explicitly cited a lack of campaign funds as a critical factor in the decision. Harris' campaign brought in $40 million, still an astronomical number to most Americans today, but in comparison to the dollars raised by her primary opponents, it was insufficient.

This enduring fundraising gap is directly tied to the historically entrenched barriers of racism and sexism that skew beliefs about who is seen as a leader. When you add the impact of the Supreme Court's *Citizens United v. Federal Elections Commission* decision, the game feels obviously rigged. In 2010, a conservative nonprofit organization, Citizens United, petitioned the Supreme Court for the right to finance and promote a film that was critical of then-Senator Hillary Clinton just before the 2008 presidential primary contests began. In a 5–4 decision, the Supreme Court sided with Citizens United, overturning not one but two precedents—one, the 100-year-old Tillman Act, which banned corporate contributions to federal elections, and another that banned corporations from distributing paid political communications in the days leading up to an election. The consequence? Political control and outcomes are now disproportionately in the hands of big business, special interest groups, and the wealthy donors who finance them. Those entities now have an unlimited financial stake in our elections, and politicians build their campaign coffers by pandering to these groups instead of prioritizing the needs of their constituents—precisely what Shirley Chisholm fought against.

The Citizens United decision opened the floodgates to dark money in politics and exacerbated the fundraising disparities impacting Black and brown candidates seeking public office. Between 2010 and 2020, $1.2 billion was donated to campaigns and political parties by the top ten donors in the nation (who are almost exclusively white men), and politically unaffiliated groups spent $4.5 billion, up from $750 million during the two decades prior. With this decision, cash on hand and end-of-quarter reports became even more significant metrics for political viability, while substance, connection to voters, and the will of the people faded further into the democratic void. These same metrics are often a death knell for Black and brown candidates and women candidates, who have historically lagged behind in fundraising and in the fight to be seen as serious political contenders.

Now, there is one anomaly in recent history, a candidate who defied the fundraising sand trap in presidential primary politics. With his charisma, impatient political agenda, and the power of the internet and social media, President Barack Obama redefined fundraising for an entire generation. His 2008 campaign tapped into young people's attunement to social and political justice, small-dollar donations, and celebrity support in a way that built upon and exponentially expanded Chisholm's approach. By June 2008, just as Obama secured enough super delegates to win the Democratic nomination, he had raised $339 million, $100 million more than Hillary Clinton, the other Democratic frontrunner at the time. These were record-setting numbers in 2008, and all before *Citizens United v. FEC* was decided in 2010. But even with his fundraising, the possibility that the majority of voters—meaning enough white voters—could see Obama as America's leader felt slim. Some Black voters communicated as much by saying, "They're not gonna let him win." But ultimately, Obama prevailed with historic margins as he secured 365 electoral votes, well beyond the 270 needed to win the presidency, and became the first Black president of the United States of America.

Today, the California fundraising swing is still a centerpiece in US politics for both Democrats and Republicans, even though the GOP makes every effort to cast Los Angeles as the ultimate West coast villains. Hollywood has been ever present in politics since the start of motion pictures, as stars, studio executives, and the staggering wealth of the entertainment industry emerged as fertile ground for donors with deep pockets on both sides of the aisle. In recent years, that core of wealth has expanded to include tech leaders in Silicon Valley.

Typically, donations from wealthy individuals and groups often come with a wish list, or rather a list of demands, of policy changes that would aid their businesses, limit their tax liabilities and federal regulatory oversight, or score their spouse or child a powerful position.

For Democrats, Barack Obama set records in 2012 as his Hollywood swing brought in just over $14 million for his run for a second term. Immediately following the historic writers and actors strikes in 2023, President Joe Biden and First Lady Jill Biden hosted seven fundraiser events in thirty-six hours in Los Angeles, pulling in more than $15 million for the 2024 reelection campaign, reportedly a record haul for a weekend of events nearly one year before the election. And while Republicans pretend to hate Hollywood and complain about Democrats fundraising with the liberal elites of California, they are in on the same activities, raising millions in donations from real estate developers, executive producers, tech leaders, and studio heads. During the 2020 election, the famed 90210 Beverly Hills zip code made it into the top three donor sources for the Trump reelection campaign, proving, yet again, that even Republicans have their finger in the Hollywood honey pot.

A Hollywood swing has been a rite of passage for candidates running campaigns for federal office, and in 1972, Diahann Carroll and Flip Wilson created that same opportunity for Shirley Chisholm. They understood that money dictates access. They understood that the playing field ought to be leveled. They understood that by putting their money where their mouths were, they lent a degree of validation to Chisholm's campaign, her platform, and her intention to recondition the nation to see women and Black people as capable, viable political leaders. Flip Wilson made a large political donation, and supported Chisholm's campaign at a moment in time when he had a lot to lose—his show, his reputation, his privacy. Still, he knew how much the nation could gain from Chisholm's candidacy and chose to participate.

In a perfect world, where cash is not king, Flip Wilson's donation would not have been the financial anchor of Shirley Chisholm's campaign. She would have received the same level of public funding as each of the other candidates, and the people would have heard her name and seen her campaign platform just as frequently as they heard and saw her opponents'. Not to mention, all of the Black and brown and women candidates who have competed in elections after Chisholm's 1972 campaign would have had a similarly leveled financial playing field if, and only if, Chisholm's call to remove all private money from politics had been applied to federal elections decades ago. Not to mention, the nation's present leadership and efficacy of democracy would look remarkably different with a greater focus on the people and their needs.

In the real world, Chisholm understood the need to play the game by the existing rules while simultaneously pushing for those rules to change. Thankfully, Flip Wilson was a donor who did not place conditions on his contributions or demand any special requests when he handed her campaign the large check. But Wilson was a rarity. As a result, the quid pro quo of fundraising targeted to the few undermines the will of the many. Chisholm knew it then, and even with her modest coffers, she fought to make a difference.

CHAPTER THREE

THE ACTIVIST

"Challenging power structures from the inside, working the cracks within the system, however, requires learning to speak multiple languages of power convincingly."

—Patricia Hill Collins,
On Intellectual Activism

Huey P. Newton, co-founder of the Black Panther Party for Self-Defense, missed his flight the day of the Welcome to Hollywood fundraiser. His journey from Oakland, California, to Los Angeles delayed, he was running extremely late that evening. But Newton was calm when his taxi pulled into the paved driveway of Diahann Carroll's Benedict Canyon mansion. This wasn't his first Hollywood soiree. He and the Black Panthers frequently attended high-profile functions hosted by celebrities and A-lister film directors who offered financial support for their community-based work. Newton's calm was also likely a learned behavior, a response to the surveillance and harassment that he and the Black Panthers had experienced in the six years since founding the organization to fight for Black liberation.

Huey P. Newton was twenty-four years old when he co-founded the Black Panther Party with Bobby Seale in October 1966. A Louisiana native and the youngest of seven children, Newton's struggling family moved to Oakland, California, when he was three years old. The family bounced from apartment to apartment during the next ten years, barely able to keep food on the table. The local public school system failed Newton; he was functionally illiterate while still being passed through each grade of school. In his memoir, *Revolutionary Suicide*, Newton wrote, "Not one instructor ever awoke in me a desire to learn more or question or explore the world of literature, science, and history. All they did was try to rob me of the sense of my own worth, and in the process they nearly killed my urge to inquire." The person who replenished and nurtured Newton's desire to learn and grow was his older brother Melvin, who had started college while Newton was in high school. Melvin would play recordings of poetry to Newton, and they'd discuss its significance. Newton also committed some of the poems to memory. He was motivated to learn how to read because he wanted to take their poetic discussions further, but he was too ashamed to ask for help. Instead, he hid in his room for hours quietly sounding out each syllable of the poems that he had memorized by ear until he could match sounds to the letters and words in Melvin's textbooks and the dictionary. Ultimately, he made up for years of public school failures by the end of his senior year of high school, stepping into a new world of thought and academic exploration.

All of Newton's childhood experiences informed the Black Panthers' Ten-Point Program, a foundational declaration of wants and beliefs for the survival and security of Black people, and people living in poverty. In 1966, 30 million people were living in poverty, including a disproportionate number of Black people. Police brutality, while not formally documented, was regularly visible on street corners in Black communities. And the Vietnam War was ramping up as the United States continued bombings and increased troop deployments. While the federal government pumped billions of dollars into the war, domestically, people suffered as their most basic needs went unmet. Newton could articulate their needs because he shared them. And not only did he understand the needs of the people, but he understood that the power of the people would drive his activism forward. These tenants served as the core of their fight to combat these issues.

Newton verbalized much of the framework as Bobby Seale transcribed and supplemented it with his own ideas. The platform started with a demand for freedom and ended with a demand for land, bread, housing, education, clothing, justice, and peace—arguably the most basic needs for any human being to simply exist. The ten points were Newton's poetic response to Black and poor people's collective deprivation and historic abuse in the United States.

The founding platform also featured a call for the end of police brutality and the creation of self-defense groups. Newton, inspired by

Malcolm X, pushed for the self-defense groups to be visibly armed. He had witnessed the limitations of the unarmed watch groups in the Watts area of Los Angeles, where police regularly harassed Black residents, and committed to leveraging California's open carry laws in his cause. This move toward armed neighborhood patrols, paired with the fact that the individual who first provided the Black Panthers with weapons was a paid informant for the Federal Bureau of Investigation (FBI), set off a red alert among law enforcement agencies at the local, state, and federal levels. The Black Panthers had a target on their backs, and within three years of founding the organization, then–FBI Director J. Edgar Hoover defined the Panthers as "the greatest threat among the Black extremist groups to the internal security of the United States."

The FBI deployed an entire playbook through the covert operations of its Counterintelligence Program (CIP) to undermine the Black Panthers and establish an unfavorable public narrative about the group. Wiretaps, trailing and monitoring, unfounded arrests, missions to infiltrate and divide their ranks, and campaigns to plant divisive rhetoric were their tools of choice, and detailed throughout the CIP's reports.

Newton's movements in late April 1972 were even documented in official files and intelligence reports by the FBI. But by that time, he had become so accustomed to these tactics that his late arrival to the Welcome to Hollywood party was likely more of a disruption for the federal agents trailing him than to Newton himself. Agents went so far as to note that Newton and his travel companions were not met by anyone at the Los Angeles Airport as they hailed a cab, and that they planned to return home that same evening. While the Panthers accepted and maneuvered around the constant monitoring and invasion of privacy, the mental and emotional impact of what

Newton and the Panthers experienced on a daily basis would surely give anyone whiplash.

Just two days before the party at Diahann Carroll's home in Los Angeles, the Black Panthers hosted an event at St. Augustine's Episcopal Church in Oakland to formally endorse Shirley Chisholm's presidential campaign. Press releases were distributed to news outlets ahead of the endorsement announcement, making local law enforcement aware of the event. Before the press conference began, police officers parked outside the church in what the Panthers interpreted as a visible show of force. This intimidation tactic prompted the Panthers to modify their program so that Newton avoided the event entirely. The Panthers hypothesized that the local police force's intention was to arrest Newton during the endorsement press conference and overtake the headline of the day from "Panthers Endorse Chisholm," which was ultimately printed in newspapers across the nation, to "Newton Arrested During Panthers' Chisholm Endorsement Event." The officers' assumed goal was to deliver a one-two punch that would embarrass Chisholm and her campaign and feed the narrative that the Panthers were a group to be feared, rather than one deeply involved in community work and voter engagement.

In Newton's place, Bobby Seale appeared alongside Shirley Chisholm's Northern California campaign coordinator, Wilson Riles Jr., to address the reporters and supporters who attended the endorsement event. Seated in front of a chalkboard lined with "Shirley Chisholm for President" bumper stickers and details about the Panthers' next food and grocery giveaway event, Seale read a prepared statement from Newton. In the statement, Newton boldly declared that Chisholm was the "best social critic of America's injustices to run for presidential office, from whatever party," and dubbed her "the People's Candidate." There was a clear synergy between Chisholm's campaign platform—which included solutions for poverty and police brutality—and the Black Panthers' original ten-point program and their new political endeavors.

As of February 1972, the Black Panthers began to redirect their focus away from armed self-defense and toward a series of community-based programs related to education, housing, food, and freedom established as an extension of their founding tenets. Their work included free breakfast and grocery programs, free health clinics and sickle cell anemia testing, and political and grassroots organizing as a means of gaining power for the Black community. In an interview with the *National Observer*, Newton described the transition, saying, "We've rejected the rhetoric of the gun; it got about 40 of us killed and sent hundreds of us to prison. Our goal now is to organize the Black communities politically."

Up until that point, the Black Panthers had rejected traditional political structures in spite of the fact that their name and logo, the sprawling Black Panther, was based on activist Stokely Carmichael's explicit mission to engage in political organizing in Lowndes, Alabama, in 1966. In the wake of the Voting Rights Act of 1965, Carmichael leveraged the SNCC network to register Black people and elect Black leaders in the majority Black county with a population of 16,000. This work was an active affront to the local Ku Klux Klansmen and white landowners, who punished and evicted Black sharecroppers for daring to exercise their right to vote. It was also a beta test for advancing Black power within electoral politics, but it took the Newton-Seale iteration of the Black Panther Party six years before bringing this mission to the forefront of their activism. This transition marked a clear intention to drive change by infiltrating a system that was not built with Black, brown, or poor people in mind but that undoubtedly dictated their collective fate in this nation.

Huey P. Newton's attendance at the Welcome to Hollywood party served as an exclamation point to the Black Panther Party's pivot into politics. And our fundraiser host, Diahann Carroll, was thrilled to welcome Newton into the fold that evening. Her excitement to meet him could have been because the meeting served as a clapback to continuous criticism from Black people who declared that her show, *Julia*, wasn't "telling it like it is." Carroll resented this sentiment with her entire being, regularly asserting in interviews that her character, and the show writ large, was an accurate representation of her own middle-class childhood. Inviting Newton into her home was a gesture that these critics probably wouldn't have expected but would have thoroughly respected, given the Black Panthers' reputation for unequivocally eviscerating anything, and anyone, that was antithetical to Black culture. Additionally, Carroll's support for the Panthers increased as they shifted from self-defense to social welfare programs, survival initiatives, and political engagement. When reporters and interviewers questioned her about the Black Panthers in the 1970s, Carroll was clear: "Their purpose is to give dignity, education, and economic opportunity to young Blacks, and that I support."

The fundraiser would also mark the first time that Huey P. Newton and Shirley Chisholm met face-to-face, two days after the Black Panthers formally endorsed her presidential campaign. The mutual respect was immediately visible as Chisholm and Newton conversed. They were not inclined to leave the crowd of Hollywood stars and power players to speak in private, as they had no ulterior motives to hide. Rather, their conversation flowed effortlessly as other party guests mingled within earshot around the black tile pool. The pair's dynamic collaboration was unexpected, yet necessary. Both leaders were committed to tapping into the power of the people to cut a new path in national politics and better the living conditions of marginalized people across the nation. For Shirley Chisholm, that meant breaking the tradition of only white men running for president and building a national coalition large enough to negotiate the addition of substantive solutions to the Democratic Party's platform. Whether it was her idea for a basic income, or her calls for the immediate withdrawal of US troops from Vietnam, Chisholm's policy proposals resonated with the marginalized because they were a direct response to their collective desperation. In fact, Chisholm's call for unity across demographics during the fundraiser echoed Newton's own endorsement statement in which he called on "every Black, poor, and progressive human being across this country to unite together, to join Sister Shirley Chisholm's campaign..." Disruptive, inclusive coalition building was at hand.

In an effort to proactively address any questions about the Black Panthers' endorsement, Chisholm told the press that their endorsement "should not be misinterpreted," emphasizing that they had a right to endorse her presidential campaign as American citizens. Chisholm insisted on reminding her existing supporters, and the nation, that the members of the Black Panther Party were citizens who had the right to be civically engaged as voters, countering the notions that they were "others" and threatening outsiders as defined by the FBI's continuous public relations campaign against them. In the months after Newton's announcement about their organizational shift, headlines ran across the nation asking, "Have the Black Panthers Really Changed at All?" Doubt was prevalent, but Shirley Chisholm was adamant about their rights and the reality of their experiences. She further humanized the Black Panthers by expressing, "What has happened to them as an oppressed group...has led them to the conclusion that perhaps with me there is hope." Chisholm's pitch to the Black Panthers was the same pitch she made to voters across the nation who wanted a new kind of leader who would shift entire systems to address their needs. It was the same call for unity to drive change via people power, and the Panthers answered the call.

In doing so, Newton and the Panthers confirmed their willingness to support a dynamic leader, regardless of that leader's gender—a notion that confounded other Black male political figures in particular. These politicians, who often ran on similar platforms of civil rights and stronger social services, had rejected Chisholm outright, immediately casting her aside. That rejection wasn't a polite "we're not interested." Rather it was a blanket "hell no" to Chisholm's right to seek the presidency. It was loud, resentful, and expressed publicly. In a *New York Times* profile about the dynamic between Chisholm and her congressional colleagues, when asked about Chisholm and her run for the presidency, "U.S. Representative Louis Stokes of Ohio... simply shrugged and laughed, while Congressman [William Clay of Missouri] answered, 'Who's Shirley Chisholm?'" In response to their comments, Chisholm told the reporter, "What makes you think Black male politicians are any different from white male politicians?... This 'woman thing' is so deep." What was particularly stinging was that Representatives Stokes and Clay were co-founders of the Congressional Black Caucus alongside Chisholm. They'd witnessed her trailblazing efforts as the first Black woman elected to Congress up close, but they took opportunities to diminish and undermine Chisholm publicly, including in the *New York Times* and in national publications that serve primarily Black audiences such as *Jet* magazine.

Similar sentiments that Chisholm shouldn't be taken seriously had percolated during the March 1972 National Black Political Convention in Gary, Indiana, just six weeks prior to the Welcome to Hollywood party. The convention saw 3,500 Black delegates from forty-four states, Washington, DC, and the US Virgin Islands convene to develop and adopt a national agenda. They aimed to outline and address the needs of Black voters ahead of the November 1972 presidential election. It was a chaotic session—priorities were unclear as attendees fought to discuss a range of ideas, such as bussing resolutions and creating a third political party, a notion that the Reverend Jesse Jackson helped to quash, though it was his own idea. Votes on substantive resolutions were delayed by hours upon hours due to procedural issues related to selecting a permanent chairman and national leadership board for the convention. By the time it came to the question of a presidential endorsement, the tensions were so high that the convention decided not to endorse any presidential candidates and tabled the endorsement process for future discussion at an unspecified time.

Shirley Chisholm and her supporters, including Representative Ron Dellums, a congressman from California and one of two members of the Congressional Black Caucus who endorsed Chisholm's campaign in January 1972, found this outcome troubling and immediately pointed to sexism as a reason for delaying discussions. Their claim was easily substantiated when one tallies the evidence of targeted attacks and statements against Chisholm leading up to the National Black Political Convention. There was the proactive effort to discredit Chisholm to the press and define her as an ineffective leader, which the head of Operation Breadbasket told the press on the eve of Chisholm's presidential campaign announcement in January 1972. Further, Richard Hatcher, mayor of Gary, Indiana, and host of the Black National Convention, expressed, on the first day of the convention, that while Black voters "on the street" wanted the convention to endorse Shirley Chisholm, he "generally has favored no endorsement of any presidential candidate." *Jet* magazine, the preeminent magazine for Black news and pop culture, even chronicled the stark shift in sentiments from just one month before the convention: "Earlier, the males whooped it up for a Black presidential candidate. Since Mrs. Chisholm entered the race, the emphasis has shifted to issues and platforms."

As Chisholm described it, there was a "machismo group [of Black men] who felt that a Black woman who didn't consult the brothers had no business running for president." Outraged by the decision at the Black National Convention to postpone endorsement discussions, Chisholm's campaign team members who attended the convention started wearing T-shirts that read, "Get your shit together." The team was fed up, and rightfully so, by these Black leaders, these Black men, who were willing to forgo endorsing any candidate to avoid simply recognizing Chisholm's historic candidacy.

The blatant disrespect, misogynoir, and political gymnastics were particularly exasperating because they came largely from the people closest to Chisholm: Black people, specifically Black men. And that rejection by one's own community carried a distinct sting that was capable of striking the soul. This treatment also explains why Chisholm repeatedly declared that she faced more criticism and vitriol for her gender than her race. Directly and indirectly, these men were asking "How dare she try to take a Black man's spot?" "How dare a woman get in our way?" But the ever-nimble Chisholm was well primed for this fight in the political arena. The same sentiments had been lobbed at her in Brooklyn, New York, in 1968 when she ran for Congress to represent the newly created 12th Congressional District. At that time, Chisholm was a New York assemblywoman who had served for four years. A well-known, well-funded civil rights leader and Black Republican named James Farmer Jr., along with a number of other Black leaders in Brooklyn, couldn't fathom the idea that a Black woman would dare take the one spot allotted to represent a majority Black and Latino district. Farmer and his consorts attempted to reduce Chisholm to a caricature of a bossy woman. Little did they know, in 1968 in the 12th Congressional District, women outnumbered men on the voter rolls 2.5 to 1. Chisholm went to work. She tapped into every women's group—from the Parent-Teacher Association to the bridge clubs—in order to reach women where they were and ask for their votes. And these women turned out for her, delivering her a win margin of more than 21,000 votes. Simply put, the power of women voters sent Chisholm to Congress.

In the face of discrimination and rejection, Shirley Chisholm turned to the community who supported her, and took a route that emphasized her willingness to establish unexpected alliances in this election. Huey P. Newton also understood this dynamic before he and the Black Panthers endorsed Shirley Chisholm six weeks after the Black National Convention. During a speaking engagement after the Welcome to Hollywood party, Newton commented, "Chisholm was unhappy that the Black bourgeoisie had rejected her, but because they rejected her, the Black Panther Party could support her." Newton's remarks rang true, as there were long-standing fissures between the Black Panther Party and Black Democrats since the Panthers were founded. Part of the tension was related to the organization's early stance on armed self-defense, and part of it was leading Black Democrats' unwillingness to change systems that didn't serve the people or their personal priorities. Ultimately, the Panthers also understood the value of independent action for the sake of driving change within their communities.

After the Welcome to Hollywood party, the Black Panthers bolstered Shirley Chisholm's 1972 presidential campaign on the ground with their voter registration efforts. Their political organizing machine was already rolling at the local precinct level. For months, the party had been working to expand their social services and programming to provide food and resources for the local community by opening precinct offices. Those offices served as locations for community members to stop by and pick up groceries or receive medical attention, and they doubled as mobilization hubs for civic engagement. The Black Panthers registered 11,000 people in Alameda County, which included Berkeley and Oakland, scooping up voters across demographics, including young voters. In a massive expansion of enfranchisement, eighteen-to-twenty-one-year-olds in the United States were, for the first time, eligible to register and vote in the 1972 general election following the ratification of the Twenty-Sixth Amendment. That year the registration period was extended to thirty days before election day. Between 1968 and 1972, voter registration in California alone jumped from 7.925 million to 9.1 million, including more than 785,000 newly registered Democrats. This was a huge opportunity for young people to voice their concerns about the world they were entering into as soon-to-be adults, and the Black liberation movement was in the thick of it with their extensive organizing skills.

Under Bobby Seale's leadership, the Black Panthers were scientific in their voter registration and precinct operations. They facilitated regular, nonpolitical interactions with potential voters, casually connecting with them in their neighborhoods and developing a rapport so strong that organizers could talk sports or ask neighbors for a cup of sugar well before asking them to vote. During their recurring "Survival Food Drives," the Black Panthers would distribute 10,000 bags of groceries, helping people complete voter registration forms as they stood in line. There was live music and entertainment to draw even bigger crowds.

As activists working with an activist candidate, the Black Panthers understood that the people would drive their collective mission forward. And the formula was clear: meet the people where they are, give them what they need in the moment with a side of joy, not empty promises, and then get them engaged long term with voter registration. This was activist organizing, a grassroots, community-driven campaign that engaged and mobilized people who were previously excluded and disengaged from politics. Ultimately, Shirley Chisholm walked away with 5 percent of the vote, outperforming expectations, having polled at less than 2 percent in the weeks leading up to the California primary election. In effect, the Black Panthers activated the community and redistributed political power.

This model of activist organizing yielded results for Chisholm's historic campaign in 1972, and it still yields results for Black women candidates competing in elections today. One eye-opening example that shook the Democratic Party to its core was the 2018 primary election, where Congresswoman Ayanna Pressley of Massachusetts' 7th Congressional District successfully challenged Michael Capuano, a ten-term Democratic incumbent (who served twenty years in Washington, DC). While Pressley, the first Black woman to serve on the Boston City Council, and Capuano, a long-serving, white male congressman, were aligned on a number of progressive policies, their campaigns differed in their approaches to attracting and engaging voters. Going into the primary election, Capuano, who over the years had amassed a wealth of relationships in Massachusetts and Washington, DC, enjoyed a number of endorsements from well-known Black leaders, including former Massachusetts governor Deval Patrick, the second Black governor in American history, and unironically, the Congressional Black Caucus. Capuano even campaigned with the late, legendary civil rights leader Congressman John Lewis.

In contrast, Pressley echoed Chisholm's campaign motif that "change can't wait," and she got to work in the community that she had served for nearly a decade as a member of the Boston City Council. Just as the Black Panthers redistributed political power by authentically connecting with disengaged members of the community, Pressley's campaign invested in conversations with thousands of parents, students, neighbors, and workers who hadn't voted in years or at all. Thanks to new technology, they could reach people online with social media and via text message. But just like Shirley Chisholm in 1968, and the Black Panthers in 1972, the most effective interactions with voters were the casual face-to-face interactions. Pressley and her campaign team knocked on voters' doors, met them at their local community centers, and spoke to them at a direct human level. There were no empty promises, only compassionate conversations about their needs as senior citizens, concerns about their children's education, or their experiences as trauma survivors. That outreach led to more than 100,000 people casting their vote in the 2018 congressional primary election, compared to the roughly 50,000 people who voted on average in the previous three primaries. The result? Pressley's landslide primary win by a margin of 17 percentage points.

Political analysts and pollsters were caught off guard by Ayanna Pressley's win over a ten-term incumbent. The key to her victory were all the voters with whom she'd spent time, who had previously been disengaged, and who had otherwise been unlikely to be included in voter rolls or to receive calls from polling firms that attempted to project the outcome of the race. Congresswoman Pressley tapped into the people to power her campaign, and she came away with a stunning win that reverberated throughout the Democratic Party. And she has maintained her commitments to her constituents, including fighting for increased wages, federal investments in quality housing, and passing legislation in support of trauma survivors.

Many incumbent Democrats pushed back against the new voices within the Democratic Party who decided to run against them in 2018. They were upset that newcomers like Pressley were breaking an unspoken, yet well-known, political rule within Democratic politics: don't challenge your own. They saw the influx of progressive candidates within the Democratic Party, including Pressley, Alexandria Ocasio-Cortez of New York, Ilhan Omar of Minnesota, Rashida Tlaib of Michigan, and others, as a threat. Chisholm would likely classify this new, young Black and brown class of elected officials as "persona non grata," because this group of leaders, like her, arrived on the national stage as disruptors and catalysts for change, upsetting the beneficiaries of the system. This fresh crop of leaders refused to wait for permission to run for office. Rather, they grasped at political opportunities that were rightfully theirs, inspiring a generation in the process. Huey P. Newton would likely categorize these elected officials as "activist leaders" because of their proximity to challenges, their willingness to put their bodies on the line during the fight, and their commitment to prioritizing their constituents over preserving antiquated power structures.

Representatives Pressley, Ocasio-Cortez, Omar, and Tlaib stood up to racist attacks from the disgraced 45th president of the United States, who told them to "go back to where they came from." And 32 million people watched President Joe Biden's 2024 State of the Union as this group of elected officials held up signs calling for a ceasefire in the Gaza Strip and for the United States to stop funding bombs and weapons for the Israeli military. They have exercised their power in a way that is rare among elected officials. They take political risks to increase public awareness, and they've inspired voters across the nation to challenge systems that have failed to meet the needs of the people. This is leadership, and it frightened the Democratic establishment.

Unfortunately, in politics, the trademark response to fear includes punitive measures. In the 1972 primary election, punishment for Chisholm's out-of-the-box campaign looked like Black Democrats' decision to disparage Chisholm in the press, and to prevent pivotal endorsements, including from the Black National Convention, all because she wouldn't "play politics the way they do."

After the 2018 primary election, it came in the form of the Democratic Congressional Campaign Committee's (DCCC) decision to create a "blacklist." The DCCC resolved to track and ban any political consultants or campaign strategists who worked with candidates seeking to challenge Democratic incumbents in Congress. The consultants, strategists, and staffers who dared to collaborate with the primary challengers would be blocked from working with other Democratic campaigns for the House of Representatives. They would also be prohibited from attending briefings and meetings hosted by the DCCC, thereby effectively being shut out from opportunities to collaborate with other DCCC-approved vendors. With these bans, the DCCC effectively said, "Unseat incumbent Democrats, and we will cut you off." And they did... at least until the blacklist was lifted following the 2020 election cycle, under the new leadership of then-Representative Sean Maloney of New York.

Just as Chisholm had lingering pain and bruises after being subjected to unfounded castigation, the damage still lingers in the form of distrust for the new generations of congresswomen. Decades after her being rejected and sabotaged by many in her own party, Chisholm described how she regularly cried because she was "misinterpreted," and how even in the midst of that painful rejection, she understood why many Black men responded to her the way they did. "... [They] felt the time had come for Black men. It was Black men's turn, and nobody should get in the way, including Black women. So, I understood that, but it was very hurting." After being abused and cast aside through the tools of systemic oppression, racism, and white supremacy, as soon as any glimmer of opportunity presented itself, Black men made the chauvinistic assumption that the opportunity belonged to them first. That sentiment was resoundingly clear during 1972, a year that represented expansive opportunity, especially in politics. The enforcement of the Voting Rights Act of 1965 was yielding increased political engagement from Black people. Not to mention, Black pride was on the rise as part of the Black liberation movement. And Chisholm understood that the notion of "Black men's turn" was rooted in the scarcity and deprivation of rights that Black people had experienced and internalized since being forced to the shores of North America. But her explicit choice to not blame these men for their own internalized hurt explains how she was able to move forward with them, even campaigning with the Reverend Jesse Jackson in 1980 when he ran for the Democratic nomination for president.

Today, these progressive congresswomen choose to keep the DCCC at an arm's length while creating their own political committees to support and endorse candidates of their choice. They balance their autonomy by advocating for, and against, actions by the Democratic Party, whether that is applauding student loan debt relief or vocally opposing the US decision to send military aid and artillery to Israel. They also fight to fill the political void that leaves many disillusioned, as 84 percent of the nation does not have trust and faith in the government.

Chisholm knew the cost of attempting to fill a political void—one that had previously ignored the contributions of women and offered Black candidates limited opportunity to effect real change. It was work that required fortitude, and being "able to withstand the insults, the humiliations, the abuses, and the slurs." But she was not made of steel. She felt each assault as a pang against her petite frame. Each affront left a scar. Thankfully, none of it hindered Chisholm's commitment to driving change forward for the people as an activist leader strengthened by other activist leaders such as Huey P. Newton and the Black Panthers.

CHAPTER FOUR

THE YOUTH

"Well, it's on you kids now; we fucked it all up, and now it's your job to fix it."

—ANONYMOUS ADULT TO X GONZÁLEZ, ACTIVIST AND PARKLAND SURVIVOR, *THE CUT*

When Barbara Lee walked into Diahann Carroll's home for the Welcome to Hollywood party, she was in work mode. Though she was likely one of the youngest people in the room, and the only student in attendance, she couldn't be bothered to soak in the sheer volume of celebrity that encapsulated her, or the lavish decor and champagne being passed among the guests. Lee was on a mission. After traveling with Huey P. Newton from Oakland, California, to Carroll's Beverly Hills home, Lee was about to formally introduce Newton to Shirley Chisholm face-to-face for the first time. Locating Chisholm in the sea of partygoers was a bit of a task for Lee as she waded into the crowd that was gathered in Diahann Carroll's lush, tree-lined backyard sanctuary. But as soon as Lee laid eyes on the presidential candidate, she made a beeline to her with Newton at her side. Finally, after hands had been shaken and Chisholm and Newton were conversing in the center of the crowd, Lee could breathe a sigh of relief.

This improbable meeting had been weeks in the making. Barbara Lee had served as the quiet bridge builder between Chisholm's presidential campaign and the Black Panthers, as she was the one who convinced Newton and Bobby Seale to take a closer look at Chisholm's platform and approach to activist leadership. After witnessing the alignment between both entities as a volunteer, Lee took the initiative to meet with Newton and Seale to gauge their interest and awareness of Shirley Chisholm's efforts. In their conversations, she emphasized Chisholm's solutions for national challenges such as the Vietnam War, poverty, and injustice. As the Panthers had recently transitioned to voter organizing efforts in Northern California, Lee also stressed how supporting Chisholm's campaign would be a valuable voter mobilization effort for the Panthers' future political prospects. It was a perfectly timed collaboration.

Today, people may recognize Barbara Lee as the courageous congresswoman who represented Oakland, California, for nearly thirty years. She has been a constant defender of the people, someone who has never backed down from doing what's right, even when she was alone in doing so. Case in point, Lee cast the singular vote in Congress against authorizing the war in Afghanistan in the days after the September 11th terrorist attack. But in 1972, Lee was a twenty-five-year-old president of the Black Student Union at Mills College and a mother of two receiving public assistance. She was also an active community worker associated with the Black Panther Party, spending her time connecting her neighbors to the Panthers' health clinics and breakfast programs.

Before joining Chisholm's campaign, Lee was also a young person who was so disillusioned with politics that she refused to register to vote. Lee did not believe that the white men leading the two-party political system understood her needs, nor were they capable of addressing the challenges facing low-income women. The early 1970s were marked by a financial crisis. More than 25.5 million people were living below the poverty line. The national unemployment rate had increased to nearly 5 percent, with Black people disproportionately unemployed at a rate of 8.5 percent. And inflation was speeding toward a historic high of 12 percent. Like many other young Black Americans, Barbara Lee was struggling. She wanted, and deserved, solutions. In the immediate moment, that included receiving free groceries from the Black Panthers, and joining advocacy efforts with other single mothers to call for additional benefits, given the rising housing and food costs of the time. Lee was trying to survive as best she could when Congresswoman Shirley Chisholm lit a political spark inside her.

As president of the Black Student Union, Lee invited Chisholm to speak at Mills College in the spring of 1972 because she was the first Black woman elected to Congress. She had no idea, at the time, that Chisholm had also launched a presidential campaign. After hearing Chisholm speak to her classmates about withdrawing US troops from the Vietnam War, the importance of a woman's right to have an abortion, and strategies to eliminate poverty with basic guaranteed family incomes, Lee was desperate to join Chisholm's campaign team. She asked the congresswoman how she could get involved and support her vision for the future of this nation, and Chisholm started at an explicitly basic first step: register to vote.

As Lee recalls, "She called me 'little girl' and shook her finger at me... she said, 'Don't you know they're making decisions about you?'... and she convinced me that [voting] will make a difference." After registering, Lee immediately got to work organizing Northern California voters and stakeholders for Chisholm. She also took it upon herself to begin having conversations with Huey P. Newton and Bobby Seale about the Black Panther Party endorsing Chisholm's campaign. In April 1972, Lee also traveled to Gary, Indiana, to represent the Chisholm campaign at the Black National Convention. Frustrated by the convention organizers' efforts to avoid a vote to endorse Shirley Chisholm, or any presidential candidate, Lee was the campaign staffer who distributed the "Get your shit together" T-shirts among Chisholm supporters to wear in protest.

Barbara Lee was out front for Shirley Chisholm, as were many young people. They were drawn to Chisholm's campaign and style of political leadership. In fact, it was the youth who challenged Chisholm to expand her own thinking around her leadership potential, planting the seed of a presidential run in her mind years earlier.

For many Baby Boomers, their first glimpse of Shirley Chisholm's leadership was in March 1969 during her inaugural congressional floor speech about the Vietnam War—the same speech that some of her colleagues said she was "crazy" to make. Walking up to the lectern on the House floor wearing her cat-eye-framed glasses and holding a stack of notes for reference, Chisholm was confident and clear as she called on the Nixon administration to flip their priorities from financing a seemingly unending war to investing in solutions that addressed education, poverty, and housing. She spoke plainly, without jargon or innuendo, a departure from the politicians who obfuscated with rhetoric and catchphrases and in turn failed to communicate any explicit push for substantive change. The congresswoman knew she was on the right side of history as she called out President Nixon and his cabinet for offering billions of dollars in funding to the Department of Defense while simultaneously claiming that they simply did not have the resources to fund educational initiatives such as Head Start. She turned the president's own words against him when she reminded her colleagues that it was Nixon who said, "When you cut expenditures for education, what you are doing is short-changing the American future." She also exposed the administration's intention to continue the Vietnam War for at least another two years, which would result in further neglect of pressing domestic issues. Chisholm then boldly promised to reject all future funding requests and appropriations legislation for the military and the Department of Defense that were brought to the House floor for a vote. After declaring her protest vote, she committed to maintaining this position until the administration shifted its financial focus back to the American people.

Chisholm's declaration was provocative and necessary. Not only did she provide her colleagues with a speech writing master class, but she also took the Nixon administration to task for their blatant refusal to fulfill their commitments and address the needs of the public. In Chisholm's choice to proactively draw the line on Defense spending bills, she made an actionable, trackable vow to her peers and to the public in opposition to the war. This transparent action represented a degree of accountability and direct communication that was scarce among elected leaders at the time. Chisholm and only three other members of the House of Representatives made this commitment, and by starting her tenure in the House on this note, she distinguished herself as a bold legislator and advocate. That day, she became a leader in the anti-war movement, and a hero in the eyes of the young people who had been calling for change and an end to the Vietnam War.

During a candid conversation with a group of middle-school-age children on the steps of Congress that same year, Chisholm was honest with them about her "mixed feelings" about being the first Black woman to serve in the House of Representatives. She noted that "as far as I'm concerned, actually, it's overdue. So, I don't get terribly excited about it." When one of the students asked her about one day running for the US Senate, Chisholm hesitated for a millisecond, breaking her usual cadence of speech as though she hadn't considered the notion before. She replied, "It would be my hope... that maybe someday I might be able to hold the seat that the late Senator Robert F. Kennedy held in New York, being the first Black woman also to come to the United States Senate."

Similarly, college students whom Congresswoman Chisholm met on her campus tours and speaking engagements began to ask her if she would one day run for president. Whenever asked, she dismissed the notion with a laugh and a comment about her race and her gender being barriers. That is, until a student asked her, "When are we going to break this tradition?"—referring to the nearly two-centuries-long tradition of white men running for and serving as president of the United States.

That single question was a jolt to Chisholm's system. She was already a known disrupter who was directly challenging policy and tradition as the first Black woman elected to the House of Representatives. She also understood that the White House dictated agendas and policy priorities in a way she and her few allies in Congress never could, especially at a moment of compounding national crises. That was why this student's query piqued her interest. In fact, without this suggestion, there would have never been a Chisholm presidential campaign.

The student then added, "We will be voting soon, and we will support you if you run," referring to the recently passed Twenty-Sixth Amendment, which would enfranchise 25 million eighteen-to-twenty-year-olds as first-time voters in the 1972 election. Chisholm was excited by the proposition of collaborating with young people as they flexed their political muscle for the first time to make their mark on American politics. She shared their urgent desire for change and was therefore a draw for the eighteen-to-twenty-nine-year-olds who had been watching her push boundaries since she entered Congress. And the timing of Chisholm's election to Congress was fortuitous as they had been in search of an authentic, powerful advocate to fill the vacuum of leadership created by the devastating assassination of Dr. Martin Luther King Jr. in April 1968, and the assassination of Senator Robert F. Kennedy just two months later. In a matter of eight weeks, two visionary leaders who had their entire lives ahead of them were struck down. Their deaths left gaping wounds in the hearts of people of all ages who had fought for better and believed that better could even be achieved in this country.

On the eve of his passing, Dr. King addressed a crowded congregation at the Bishop Charles Mason Temple in Memphis, Tennessee, in support of the city's sanitation workers, who were on strike, and calling for increased wages and improved working conditions. In his speech, Dr. King reaffirmed his belief that the marches, strikes, and protests would lead to a higher quality of life for Black people, and that our collective survival as human beings demanded that we fight to secure human rights in spite of the threats. Tragically, Dr. King also predicted that he "may not make it to the promised land." He was assassinated the next afternoon. As Senator Kennedy announced Dr. King's death to a crowd from the back of a pickup truck in a dark field in Indianapolis, Indiana, he pronounced his heartbreak through the existential question: "In this difficult time for the United States, it's perhaps well to ask what kind of a nation we are and what direction we want to move in."

By the late 1960s and into the 1970s, political violence and war were two defining issues for the Baby Boomer generation. In addition to Dr. King's and Senator Robert Kennedy's assassinations, this generation faced military conscription, otherwise known as the draft, and the vicious death rates of the Vietnam War. By 1970, 1.53 million Americans had been drafted to serve in Vietnam, 48,736 US troops had been killed, and an indeterminate number of civilians in Northern Vietnam, Southern Vietnam, Cambodia, and Laos had been killed.

In the midst of young people's collective rage, these traumas and losses activated their survival instinct. Having witnessed the civil rights movement and experienced the cultural rebellion of drugs and rock music, they were equipped with the tools of protest as they rejected the status quo and fought for their lives and their rights. That desperation was what made that generation so powerful, and they have begrudgingly passed down that power to their grandchildren.

The visceral scene of students and protesters scrambling across grassy quads or down unfamiliar streets to escape law enforcement with guns drawn and fumes spewing from tear gas canisters sadly, and unsurprisingly, spans generations. This reality is captured in the images of Baby Boomers protesting the Vietnam War on a grass-covered hill at Kent State in 1970. National guardsmen walked toward the protesters in a line formation and fired their weapons into the crowd, killing four people and wounding nine others. The scene repeated as their grandchildren protested George Floyd's murder at the hands of a Minneapolis police officer in 2020 in cities across the nation. In Washington, DC, tear gas filled the streets surrounding the White House, as US Army helicopters flew within 100 feet of protesters' heads, and police in riot gear beat back crowds with batons. And in 2024, the scenes from the anti-war protests on college campuses in twenty-six states and Washington, DC, again gave witnesses a sense of nauseating nostalgia. In particular at Columbia University, where New York City police were deployed to remove student encampments, drive an armored tank onto the campus, and arrest students and protesters who occupied an administrative building.

The 2024 protests were a direct response to the Israeli bombardment of the Gaza Strip with US-supplied weapons and munitions. The bombing began in the weeks following the October 7, 2023, attack by Hamas, a militant group and US-designated foreign terrorist organization, which was elected into power in Gaza in 2006. Hamas' attack resulted in 1,200 Israeli and dual citizens being killed, and hundreds more being kidnapped. Video footage of the attack showed bleeding civilians being forced into vehicles, running in panic, and being shot and killed. In response, on October 27, 2023, Israel launched air strikes into the Gaza Strip with the communicated goal of eradicating Hamas. However, Palestinian civilians were killed in droves with each strike, often in large family groups. Images captured the death and devastation as schools, hospitals, mosques, and United Nations facilities—all locations where civilians sheltered—were bombed. Israel also blocked humanitarian aid from reaching the territory, and forced millions of Palestinian civilians to migrate south in search of refuge as their tanks advanced into all corners of the Gaza Strip. According to reports in May 2024, more than 34,000 Palestinians were killed, more than 78,000 Palestinians were wounded, and nearly 2 million were displaced. The college students and organizers were calling for an end to the war in Gaza and demanding that their universities divest from Israel.

The parallels between the protests in 1970 and those of the 2020s showcased the damning repetition of history. Even fifty years later, as people in their late teens and early twenties organized and led marches, local and state leaders escalated with militarized responses from law enforcement. They threatened to call in the national guard if the crowds refused to disperse, and thousands of students, professors, and protesters were arrested. However, the new generation of protesters leveraged new tools such as the internet and the presidential primary election to raise awareness globally.

Generation Z broadcasted their revolution. They recorded and shared footage to expose inhumane treatment in real time as their tent encampments were flooded by sprinklers in the middle of the night in near-freezing temperatures. They shared footage of a Texas organizer instructing his peers on how to safely disperse from a campus quad, as law enforcement had directed them to, only for him to be thrown to the ground and arrested. Sharing these images online for the world to see allowed for a layer of protection for protesters, and accountability for leaders and law enforcement. This was likely a lesson learned from the protest movements in the 2010s, including the Arab Spring (the anti-government uprisings in Tunisia, Egypt, Libya, and throughout the region in 2011), and the protests following police shootings of unarmed Black people, as in Ferguson, Missouri, after the 2014 killing of Michael Brown.

In a separate electoral push, "anti-war, pro-peace" organizers quickly developed the Listen to Michigan campaign during the 2024 presidential primary election. The campaign demanded change in how the United States engaged with Gaza and Israel in a language that political power players and Democratic operatives understood: withholding votes. Similar to the Black Panthers, the Listen to Michigan campaign operated within the conventional political system to activate, build community, and demonstrate the electoral power of voters who opposed the Biden administration's handling of Israel's bombardment of Gaza. The key protest action here was for voters to cast an "uncommitted" vote on their primary ballots to pressure the administration to call for an immediate ceasefire, and to stop sending munitions and resources to Israel. As this ballot protest occurred during the primary election, each "uncommitted" voter represented what the Democratic Party stood to lose, and the stakes were clear, given the limited margins of Joe Biden's win during the 2020 presidential election against Donald Trump.

The 2020 election was uncomfortably close, especially in the battleground states that could make or break a candidate's ability to win the 270 electoral votes needed to secure the presidency. In Michigan, Biden beat Trump by only about 150,000 votes. In Pennsylvania, Biden beat Trump by 80,500 votes. And in Wisconsin,

Biden beat Trump by 20,600 votes. Originally, organizers in Michigan hoped for 10,000 voters to cast uncommitted ballots, and they did not have plans to expand the effort—that is, until the numbers were reported. The Listen to Michigan campaign earned 101,000 "uncommitted" votes, a feat that captured national attention. Buoyed by voter engagement and excitement, the campaign spread to the nine states where "uncommitted" is a ballot option, and to dozens of states where organizers used write-in campaigns to register anti-war voter dissent. As the primaries progressed, the "uncommitted" effort earned 61,000 votes in Pennsylvania, and 48,300 votes in Wisconsin, and ultimately earned nearly two dozen delegates to attend the Democratic National Convention. The youth led the charge.

After eighteen-to-twenty-nine-year-old voters turned out en masse to deliver history-defying results for Democrats in the 2022 midterm elections, the Democratic Party was caught off guard as their youngest supporters leveraged a tool of democracy against an incumbent Democratic president during a presidential election cycle. But more important than maintaining political traditions and decorum, young people knew that they had to fight hard to demand more and better from their elected leaders.

That concept of "more and better" extends beyond the anti-war movement to include the shortcomings of democracy and the threats to their day-to-day lives. Threats like how billionaire donors have a bigger role in selecting presidents than voters do through unchecked campaign contributions. Like a rogue Supreme Court that rejected fifty years of precedent to end access to abortion, gutted the Voting Rights Act, and granted blanket immunity to the man who attempted to overturn the results of the 2020 presidential election. There's also the coordinated state legislative voter suppression effort that has led twenty-nine states to pass restrictive laws since November 2020, and anti-LGBTQ legislation that has been passed in twenty-two states as of June 2024. When it comes to simply existing, trauma has followed this generation at every stage of development. As toddlers, the September 11th terrorist attacks upended national security and fed global conflict. As elementary school students, the recurring drills expanded from fire drills to active shooter drills as mass school shootings became more frequent, and access to guns and military-style weapons expanded. They have had the internet at their fingertips throughout their adolescence, and while being online has expanded their global connectivity, it has had an overwhelmingly negative impact on their mental health. As high school and college students, they've experienced a global pandemic that restricted their daily lives to being exclusively online for a year. And any thoughts about their future remains shrouded in fears about climate change (which one political party refuses to acknowledge as a real threat).

It's no wonder Generation Z wants to throw the entire system away. They have suffered compounding losses, and now they want proof that politics and government can yield something positive in their lives. Ultimately, the feelings of Gen Z are virtually identical to the feelings of Barbara Lee in 1972. She refused to register to vote because she didn't believe the elected leaders adequately represented who she was or understood what she needed. She didn't trust the government. And she didn't believe that the two-party system could yield presidential candidates who were capable of responding to her needs. In both 1972 and 2024, those needs were a matter of life and death, and global in scale. These conditions are what prompt young people's willingness to reject norms and create a new way forward.

What's most jarring about this reality is that after their elders and parents raised this generation to dream and be anything they could imagine, they quickly attempt to implement guardrails when their children and grandchildren's ideas go beyond what they themselves believed to be possible. Or they dismiss the youth's push for change as unreasonable and impossible. It's similar to Barbara Lee's ability to persuade the Black Panthers to endorse Shirley Chisholm's campaign after she was rejected by established Democrats, and the success of the Listen to Michigan campaign's uncommitted movement during the 2024 presidential primary. Young people acted out of necessity, and established political players attempted to cry foul because the actions were creatively unexpected and highly effective in power building. Thankfully, the young people in both scenarios were undeterred, but if they had been, it would have negatively impacted our broader society and our democracy. Not to mention, that deterrence is the opposite of how Shirley Chisholm engaged with young people.

Chisholm understood the angst of young people largely because she shared their sentiments of frustration and outrage when it came to the inefficiencies and hollow platitudes of government. A government that failed to deliver anything of substance for a people who were struggling, no less. That angst was reflected in her direct tone, her public declarations and commitments, and her willingness to engage them substantively. It fed her just as it feeds young people today.

All they want is a leader who is authentic, willing to listen and learn, and can provide tangible solutions. Someone who is willing to be in the trenches of their reality alongside them, without judgment or condescension. Someone who is welcoming of their push to challenge tradition in the name of developing humane, inclusive policies. That's why Barbara Lee went above and beyond for Shirley Chisholm, and it's also why young people implanted the notion of a historic role for Chisholm. The next generation of leaders will have to exude and practice this behavior authentically if they want any shot at appealing to Gen Z, or even Generation Alpha. Because one way or another, the young people will force this nation forward with the frame of "help us or get out of the way."

CHAPTER FIVE

THE MEDIA

"The press is so powerful in its image-making role, it can make a criminal look like he's the victim and make the victim look like he's the criminal. This is the press."

—MALCOLM X, "SPEECH AT THE AUDUBON BALLROOM"

"TELL ME, DO YOU THINK THERE CAN EVER BE A WOMAN President of the United States?"

David Frost, the legendary English journalist and interviewer extraordinaire, swiveled in his orange chair and leaned toward Shirley Chisholm as he posed this question ever so coolly. It was the fall of 1969, and a presidential bid was not yet on Chisholm's radar. She hadn't even served a full year in Congress as the freshman from New York who was carving out a lane for Black women in the then-180-year-old political institution. Still, she was full of spunk and spirit as she smiled and settled into the one-on-one interview with Frost on the set of his newly syndicated television show, *The David Frost Show*.

Frost was a relative newcomer to American audiences when he launched his ninety-minute US-based program in the summer of 1969. But across the pond, in the United Kingdom, Frost's popularity was off the charts. All the Brits knew David Frost, as his name recognition was second only to the prime minister. His career had been on the rise since 1962, when he gained appeal and acclaim on the satirical, week-in-review BBC show *That Was the Week That Was*. His success on that project led to the creation of *The Frost Report*, another comedy news show, in March 1966, and *The Frost Programme*, a more serious interview-based show, in December 1966. Frost was introduced to American audiences by way of a US version of *That Was the Week That Was*, and he reappeared on US screens for a series of interviews he conducted with American presidential candidates during the 1968 election. David Frost's ambitious nature ensured that his schedule was jam-packed on both continents. By the summer of 1969, Frost's weekly schedule included filming in New York on Mondays, Tuesdays, and Wednesdays, before catching a red-eye flight to London to film on Fridays, Saturdays, and Sundays. The sleep deprivation and trans-Atlantic routine seemed to fuel Frost, rather than deplete him, as he seemed to command his body to function on the sheer excitement of his career expansion.

Frost sought to import his interview style with his new US show, highlighting "things in America that Americans take for granted..." Those "things" included the mundane, like complimentary matchbooks at restaurants (which Frost was confounded by), to the striking and overwhelmingly intimate, like multiple guests disclosing their vasectomy surgeries on-air months apart. It was a testament to his ability to create an environment of warmth and welcome at the Little Theatre in Midtown New York City. Even with the minimalist setup of two to three armchairs—a blatant rejection of the traditional interview couch and oversized host desk—the set design allowed a closeness to the audience and the guests to shine. Frost also raised the stage on a maroon-colored platform so that he could walk to the edge, sit on the step, and engage audience members throughout his interviews. All of this was wrapped in three walls that were lined with orange, maroon, and purple panels.

The flow of guests varied—from Yoko Ono and John Lennon, who threw acorns into the audience and encouraged people to plant them and grow trees in their community; to four-time Olympic gold medalist Jesse Owens, who summed up his interactions with Adolf Hitler during the 1936 Olympics, saying, "I didn't go over there to shake hands with him. [The American athletes] went to run, and run we did. We had a marvelous time, so sorry that he didn't." Then there was the rousing interview with Lucille Ball and Carol Burnett. When Frost questioned Ball about the public perception that women aren't funny, Ball adjusted her dress and played with her hair. The audience howled after she leaned forward with a blank stare and responded, "I didn't even hear you. What'd you say?"

In addition to his natural ability to embrace unexpected moments with his interview subjects, Frost also made every effort to dedicate airtime to esteemed guests from traditionally marginalized groups. His goal of platforming topics and themes that Americans took for granted was achieved in these long-form interviews. He featured Reverend Jesse Jackson in a conversation about police brutality and his vision for protecting Black communities. As the women's liberation movement took hold, he talked with Gloria Steinem about the value of women's work inside and outside of the home, and the value of choice in every part of a woman's life. Frost signed off on every single guest who appeared on his ninety-minute program, a list that included James Baldwin, Dick Gregory, and Stokely Carmichael. Frost featured these guests with the deep understanding that each editorial decision for his show, or in any newsroom or media organization, is aligned with an agenda, no matter how overt or subliminal. He believed that these individuals' stories were just as important as others dominating news cycles, and he intentionally created a new, safe space for his unique roster of interview subjects in the American media landscape. Frost's gift, years before his infamous interview with disgraced former president Richard Nixon, was wielding the power of the media.

The media cast its powerful spotlight upon Shirley Chisholm after she entered Congress in 1969, and it created a harmful glare. Unfortunately, her characterization as an angry, difficult Black woman aligned with some of the tropes and depictions of Black women in the late 1960s and early 1970s. The Sapphire trope—that Black women were loud, angry, and rude—was based on a character created by two white male actors for the minstrel radio show *Amos 'n Andy* in 1928. This distilled characterization also appeared in the behaviors of Flip Wilson's drag character, Geraldine, as she would cut her eyes in disdain at guests, raise her voice in frustration, or whoop loudly at her own jokes during sketches. The media leaned on this trope when reporting about Chisholm's request for a new congressional committee assignment. The *Boston Globe* declared that Chisholm was "incensed" when she "revolted against" her assignment to the House Agriculture Committee and Forestry Subcommittee as a first-term congresswoman by "striding up to the microphone," and "refusing to budge" until leadership recognized her. These were some of the first stories that the nation read about Chisholm's leadership in Congress, and it dictated the public's opinion about her. Even years before as an assemblywoman in the New York State Assembly, she had been dubbed "militant" by the Associated Press.

While the media depicted Chisholm as a negative force in Congress, there were other stereotypes about Black women that were harder to assign to Chisholm, such as Black women being depicted as "welfare women" who were "less inclined" to try to find work, and any oversexualized characters, as featured in the new frontier of Blacksploitation films. Though Chisholm's family received welfare benefits throughout her childhood, she had been instilled with a strong work ethic and discipline. While she worked as a teacher during the day, she attended courses at Columbia University at night as part of a master's degree program. There was no way the media could box her in as lazy and unmotivated. When it came to being oversexualized, Chisholm neutralized this notion with her uniform of a modest shift dress, horn-rimmed glasses, and a tightly curled, rounded wig. She dressed for comfort, convenience, and with a clear indicator that she was about her business. The closest the media came to this trope was in a *Boston Globe* headline that declared Chisholm was "Congress' Pepperpot," though the writer quickly defined that term as a "system-bucker," and "trouble-shooter."

Shirley Chisholm was a dynamic, intellectual woman with vision. She transcended politics to permeate culture, though the mass media depictions in 1969 would have you believe that she couldn't possibly possess those qualities essential for effective leadership. David Frost created an opportunity for Chisholm to challenge these notions on television with an extended, human-centered interview.

From start to finish, Chisholm stayed centered in herself. She was clear and authentic, as well as warm and charming. For his part, Frost matched her energy and egged her on as the conversation flowed with laughter, and the two leaned in like old friends sharing secrets. There was no rushing this long-form interview as the nation got an introduction to Chisholm beyond what they had read in the headlines. And despite whatever the public felt about seeing a Black woman directly challenging white men on the public record in Congress, her image and distinct voice were transmitted into millions of televisions. In 1969, 95 percent of American households owned a television, and *The David Frost Show* was syndicated and distributed to stations across the nation. The public could see Shirley Chisholm up close, not as a figurehead and not an abstract history maker, but as a human being. Her dynamism shone through as she discussed her personal life, her love of the arts, and the daily exercise of navigating machismo, sexism, and racism as the first Black woman elected to the United States Congress.

When it came to debates in Congress, Chisholm candidly expressed to Frost that her colleagues were filled with contempt each time she publicly outdid them with her arguments and evidence during interactions on the House floor. "In fact, one man had the nerve to say to me, 'I don't believe you're really human.'" By rejecting her humanity and her gender, she could only be an alien in their minds. Because in what world would a Black person and a woman be superior to them in any way? And how many others could possibly duplicate Chisholm's efforts and energy in the future? Dismissing Chisholm as otherworldly allowed her male counterparts to marginalize her potential impact in their shared profession.

When Frost inquired about Chisholm's tactics for navigating Congress, and piercing through her colleagues' resistance so that they could negotiate bills, she described the lore of the infamous Washington, DC, cocktail parties. The cocktail parties were where Chisholm was able to get down to business and reach her more powerful colleagues, who were at other times closed off and opposed to her point of view. Her focus in these social environments enabled her to outmaneuver her male peers in a relaxed way, allowing her to garner their support. The free-flowing drinks certainly didn't hurt either. Chisholm told Frost that she would move in as her colleagues were "freer," which prompted Frost to ask for an invitation to the next cocktail party to watch her in action. The live studio audience laughed, affirming Frost's request.

When asked about her support system, Chisholm revealed that her husband of nineteen years, Conrad Chisholm, was "...one of the most marvelous persons." She described how grateful she was that Conrad was a strong man who wasn't threatened by her abilities and ambitions like other men were. Instead, he supported her, having witnessed her impact and "how people, both Black and white, have come asking you to give them leadership." Conrad Chisholm was indeed a rarity. He championed Chisholm's political aspirations at a time when others questioned her sanity and her womanhood simply for the fact that she wanted to fight for better for her community. So when Chisholm answered the people's call to serve and to lead, it was an easy choice for Conrad to stand beside her, and behind her—both positions equally important. Beside her, he defended her from naysayers who declared that she was meant to be at home tending to his needs, and he was her confidant who understood her pain. Behind her, he could support her and observe her, noticing things she ignored, including a growing tumor that led to her hospitalization during her congressional campaign in 1968.

For the big finale of the interview, David Frost had a surprise. He had a grand piano wheeled out to the stage. It's likely that most viewers, in the studio audience and at home, had no idea about Chisholm's artistic talents. She played the piano, she was a dancer, she designed clothing, and she wrote poetry. This interview with Frost gave her the chance to spotlight her nine years of childhood piano lessons taken on a $25 piano her parents scrounged to purchase for her. Her performance did not disappoint. Chisholm opted for a jazz number, a callback to her rebellious youth when she played jazz by ear in spite of her mother's explicit insistence that she only learn classical piano. Taking a seat at the piano, Chisholm "pounded out 'Tuxedo Junction,'" and the crowd cheered as the smooth melody filled the studio. Frost was so excited by her performance that he invited her back to play again.

Shirley Chisholm's invigorating appearance on *The David Frost Show* made its way across the nation, airing in different cities and towns during the next few months as stations purchased the syndicated episode. Given the positive reactions to the Frost interview, additional news specials and profiles were released about Chisholm, which told more relatable, human stories about her commitment to serving the people and her feelings as the first Black woman elected to Congress. NBC released a thirty-minute documentary that aired later in the fall of 1969, and the *Boston Globe* published a profile the following summer that emphasized Chisholm's artistry and personality. At last, she had broken through, and she was able to establish an authentic baseline for the American people to better understand who she was, and why she worked as tirelessly as she did.

Considering the depth and range of the connection during Frost and Chisholm's first meeting on the set of his show, one would imagine that when they connected again three years later at Diahann Carroll's home for the Welcome to Hollywood party, the warmth and mutual respect was high. By April 1972, two months before the California presidential primary, Chisholm's campaign was polling in single digits, and the media coverage was largely mocking toward her campaign. As she declared on the trail, "We are entering a new era" of politics, the *Philadelphia Inquirer* described her statement as "jut-jawed," and her campaign as "frivolous." Nonetheless, Chisholm's presidential campaign represented the first steps toward answering Frost's uncanny question about there ever being a woman president.

As of 1972, Frost was still living a transatlantic life hosting shows in the US and the UK. And his professional success was matched by his personal joy as he was rumored to be engaged to our glamorous host, Diahann Carroll, whom he had been dating for more than a year. The pair met after one of Carroll's live performances at the Ambassador Hotel in Los Angeles in 1970. There was an immediate attraction between the two, although they were each accompanied by their own dates that evening. Undeterred and entirely unembarrassed, they flirted while shooting pool until the early hours of the morning, when they arranged a second meeting. Interestingly enough, that second encounter happened live and on-air for *The David Frost Show*, where Frost charmed Carroll into speaking about some of her most personal experiences as a performer and about her relationship with her parents. This seems to be Frost's forte: getting to the human core of extraordinary people in the most complimentary fashion. In fact, Carroll described the intimate interview in her memoir years later as, "more like a couple getting to know each other on a first date than a network television interview." Their relationship quickly blossomed into stealing moments between filming their shows on two different continents, jet-setting to islands for weekend vacations, and enjoying holidays together in the UK. Their relationship was also high-valued fodder for the tabloids. The media craved as many details about their relationship as possible, and they used their imaginations to fill in the gaps. Before the relationship was confirmed, *Jet* magazine reported that the pair was seen on a beach in Hawaii and declared that they "looked in love." The press also erroneously decided that a diamond-encrusted "Love" pendant that Carroll wore on her mink stole was a substitute for an engagement ring—further proof that you can't believe everything that is printed.

In their private circles, the couple was more open and unguarded. Carroll and Frost loved entertaining guests and friends, and frequently co-hosted dinner parties. By the time of the Welcome to Hollywood party, the two had a fine-tuned routine as co-hosts. Carroll would select the Baccarat goblets, the Waterford China, the silver, the flowers, and the table linens, while Frost would select the menu and the wine pairings. Surprisingly, though, within their relationship, Frost was more of a social butterfly than Carroll, often urging her to extend their nightcaps with friends or linger at parties for another hour or two, which she found to be irritating on occasion. Frost loved the company, because it fed his curious appetite. Trying to imagine Diahann Carroll being ready to leave a function and her beau telling her, "Just a second, darling," brings to mind the scene-stealing deathly stares that audiences saw from Dominique Deveraux on *Dynasty*, flipping her fur over her shoulder and daring anyone around her to escalate the drama.

Given Frost's love of entertaining, it made sense that he considered himself to be the third, unofficial host of the party alongside Diahann Carroll and Flip Wilson. He must have felt right at home in Carroll's Benedict Canyon mansion, circulating among the guests, making conversation with the executives and stars, and reconnecting with acquaintances who had previously appeared on his television show.

Another guest that evening who had an eye-opening interview with Frost just a year prior, in May 1971, was none other than Huey P. Newton. The internal FBI reports would have you believe that Newton attempted to avoid all of Frost's questions during his appearance on *The David Frost Show*, and that he "talked around" every topic that Frost raised. But the reality was that Frost gave Newton the space, without interruption, to communicate exactly what the Black Panther Party represented at that time, and their mission of community service. Just as he had done for Shirley Chisholm, Frost created an open dialogue on national television for a person whom many people had their minds made up about based on the news reports. In doing so, he presented viewers with an unfiltered reality of who Newton was and what he stood for, even delving into philosophical elements that served as guiding concepts for the then-twenty-nine-year-old Newton.

When Frost asked, "Do you think that all policemen are pigs?" Newton was clear in stating that he seldom used that word, but he also recognized the value of the term in the early days of the Black Panthers. "It's a word that the Black Panther Party coined. It drew a fine line between the aggressor and the victim." He went on to explain how the term leveraged Nietzsche's concept of the power of language, and how different classes "create the language for their own perpetuation and their benefit." Newton's philosophy-based rationale and response surprised Frost so much so that he quipped, "I must say that was a sensational and indeed evolved answer. If anyone had said we were gonna get into Nietzsche in the middle of an answer about that..." Newton offered a half apology as more of a signal for Frost to keep up. In that moment, Frost's shock exposed his own preconceived notions about Newton, what he expected Newton to say, and how he expected Newton to think.

It's likely that Frost expected that Newton had a score to settle after Frost's recent interview with the Black Panther Party's attorney, Charles Garry. Newton had been somewhat frustrated by Garry's televised arguments about police killing members of the Black Panthers, and he was committed to setting the record straight for Frost and the public. He did just that. In fact, he did so well that Frost ended the interview by declaring, "We hear a lot *about* the Black Panthers but we don't hear a lot *from* them very often, and I must say what we've heard from you is very different from a lot we've heard about you." Frost had offered Newton a platform to communicate directly with a national audience in an open and nonconfrontational way, human to human. And similar to Chisholm, Newton undermined the dominant headlines and media narrative of the time, which have since, in Newton's case, been confirmed to be part of a sinister public campaign spearheaded by the FBI to sow discord among the Panthers and fear within the public.

Even when officials occupying the highest levels of the federal government are not actively plotting against Black leaders and activists, media bias continues to be a pervasive issue, especially for Black and brown communities and leaders. According to a 2023 Pew survey, 90 percent of Black people see racist news coverage "sometimes or fairly often," and 63 percent of Black Americans today believe that news about Black people is more negative than coverage of other racial communities. As one survey respondent succinctly stated, "There's not a lot of African American coverage unless it's February or it's criminal." This coverage comes about by way of a number of factors, including uninformed journalists, predominantly white newsrooms, and a lack of historical awareness of Black and brown communities. The resulting harmful narratives that are released by the media pervade the individual psyches of Black people—prompting negative impacts on self-esteem, self-worth, and capabilities, and reaffirming negative stereotypes and racist beliefs about their community. It's no wonder that, when Black Americans see and feel the racist, discriminatory framing at such a high frequency, many have come to reject traditional mainstream media outlets.

And the harmful coverage worsens when social media is factored in, as digital platforms are where hate speech and misinformation flow largely unchecked. Think back to the 2020 presidential election and the online hatred that then-Senator Kamala Harris faced after she was announced as Joe Biden's vice presidential pick, the first Black woman, and first South Asian person, to appear on a major party's presidential ticket. While many Black and brown people, women, and organizers celebrated Harris' selection, Republicans did their damnedest to put Harris in what they deemed to be her place.

When it comes to policy, there were reasonable discussions and criticisms that the public had about Harris' previous prosecutorial work, but substantive discussions were not the goal of the GOP. Their goal was, and still is, cruelty, battery, and dehumanizing a Black woman. They attacked Harris' career, claiming that she didn't earn her promotions. They attacked her disposition, attempting to paint her as an angry Black woman. They attacked her name, refusing even to pronounce it correctly, blatantly disregarding the appropriate pronunciation even when they were told on-air. They even attacked her heritage as Republican extremists revived unfounded, xenophobic birtherism claims (similar to the claims lobbed against Barack Obama) and doubts about her eligibility to be elected vice president as she is the daughter of Indian and Jamaican immigrants.

The extremist anti-Black, anti-woman, anti-immigrant core of the Republican Party was at full tilt, and there was no limit for the vitriol. Unfortunately, mainstream media echoed the false claims even as they attempted to dispel them, which compounded the harm and impact. An NBC article featured the "angry Black woman" trope in its headline, a *Wall Street Journal* piece quoted Trump calling Harris a "mad woman" in the headline, and the *New York Times* questioned her voice and her name in the headline of a piece outlining GOP attacks. In response, Harris' supporters organized efforts to combat the disinformation about her by leveraging on-air segments to amplify her efforts and pivot the conversation back to substance. Conversely, the GOP was hell-bent on waging a war against a woman simply because they did not like her taking up space in their historically white, historically male political system. And this treatment runs parallel to the treatment that historically targeted and marginalized groups continue to face at all levels of elected and public-facing leadership across industries when they dare to step up to the plate.

The pain and trauma of dehumanizing attacks leaves scars. Some will argue these attacks are simply the cost of being "the first," but the truth is that no one deserves to be stripped of their humanity by another group seeking superiority. For Harris, it came from white supremacists and misogynists in the Republican Party. For Chisholm, it came from white supremacists, misogynists, Black men, and Democrats, and it all yields an unfathomable affliction that reverberates through the initial subject and into the broader society. It's a wonder so many Black and brown people who achieve "firsts" are still standing, still leading, and still fighting.

While Shirley Chisholm did not have to confront harmful rhetoric on the internet in 1972, she did have to contend with being erased and omitted from the presidential primary campaign altogether. Media outlets seemed to repeatedly lose her invitation in the mail when it came to debates and interviews. The network executives and producers unilaterally decided that Chisholm's campaign did not warrant equal coverage or a position on the debate stage. Chisholm was ultimately elbowed out in a move by the major networks—ABC, NBC, and CBS. The three networks had set aside airtime for two of her primary opponents to participate in a series of one-on-one debates in the final six weeks before the June 1972 California primary. Chisholm was notably missing from the debate lineup, a decision that violated the federal equal time law. Somehow information about the scheduled debate leaked. Though Chisholm wrote in *The Good Fight*, "...I am not sure the full story of how it happened ever became public," one has to wonder if an advocate like David Frost or Flip Wilson flagged the networks' decision to exclude Chisholm. As a legally qualified candidate for the Democratic nomination for the presidency, Shirley Chisholm had a right to equal airtime offered to any other competing candidates according to the Federal Communications Act of 1934. A "legally qualified candidate" is a person who has publicly announced their campaign, satisfied the state and federal laws to hold said office, and qualifies for a place on the ballot, or is running a substantial write-in campaign. In spite of this legal distinction, the networks violated the FCC rules when they did not entertain Chisholm's requests to be included in the scheduled debates, or comparable programming on the networks. Being excluded from these media events put Chisholm and voters at a disadvantage. Chisholm wouldn't be able to share her campaign agenda in front of a national audience, nor would she have the opportunity to question the other candidates on how they planned to deliver on their promises for the people if elected. The networks' omission of the sole woman and the sole Black presidential primary candidate meant that the voters wouldn't be able to hear from Chisholm and that their voting decisions would be based on incomplete information.

It is also striking that Senator McGovern didn't speak up for Chisholm in this process after he'd been unceremoniously omitted by the media in the past. During the 1968 presidential primary election, McGovern had to fight for a spot on the debate stage when CBS attempted to exclude him. That election cycle, network executives didn't consider him to be a serious enough candidate to appear in a televised debate with the two front-runners. Yet he did not come to Chisholm's aid in 1972.

One person who was watching the situation and willing to stand up for Chisholm was Tom Asher, a Maryland attorney and founder of the Washington, DC, firm Media Access Project, which was dedicated to making media accessible to all. After requesting, and being denied, a space at the debates that the major networks were scheduling, Shirley Chisholm contacted Asher and initiated legal proceedings against the networks for violating the Federal Communications Act of 1934. She was ready to fight for the equal airtime that she deserved as a legally declared candidate for the Democratic nomination for president. Still, the decision-makers involved in the matter were surprised by the legal challenge. "They never dreamt that I was gonna take the case all the way to court." The "they" Chisholm was referring to likely included both the networks' leadership teams, who attempted to apply their own interpretation of the law in order to exclude Chisholm, and the Federal Communications Commission (FCC), which seemed at the ready to do the networks' bidding. Thankfully, their opinions on Chisholm, which were likely informed by the months of negative press questioning Chisholm's leadership and political prospects, were irrelevant in this legal matter. The law was clear.

In their arguments, the networks maintained that their programming choices did not violate Federal Communications Commission rules because they didn't consider the head-to-head moderated question-and-answer sessions between the two white male Democratic primary candidates to be "debates." That argument was embarrassingly lazy as the "debates" had been publicized and branded as such in newspapers across the nation.

In that first lawsuit to the FCC, the commissioners sided with the networks and rejected Chisholm's appeal for equal time. Undeterred, Asher immediately appealed the case to the DC Circuit Court of Appeals only days before the final California debate, and a three-judge panel unanimously overturned the FCC's original order, siding with Asher and Chisholm. In the decision, ABC was ordered to either invite Chisholm to participate in the scheduled television appearance with the other Democratic primary challengers, or offer her thirty minutes of free airtime. Similarly, CBS was ordered to provide her with thirty minutes of free airtime to deliver a speech. NBC was not included in the appeal decision because they had already granted Chisholm a separate interview on the *Today Show*. Chisholm was on the campaign trail addressing a church congregation in New Jersey when she received news of the ruling. "I have won another victory," she declared triumphantly to the crowd. That she did. She fought for her space, space that was rightfully hers to occupy, and space that would impact voters' choices in the election. In doing so, she set yet another precedent on fair access and coverage in the media for Black, and women, presidential candidates.

When she won the case, she was prepared to go on-air. Only two days after the ruling, Chisholm joined the other candidates for a special episode of ABC's *Issues and Answers*, and though she was the only candidate to appear remotely from New York City, Chisholm again made her mark before a national television audience. During the one-hour special, she called out the media and the public for dismissing her campaign as a joke. She reaffirmed her position against the war in Vietnam, calling for the immediate removal of troops—a position one of her opponents commended her for—and made it clear that she would be pushing for the needs of the people in policy negotiations at the Democratic Convention. Chisholm presented voters with an authentic experience of what it meant to have a woman, a Black person, and a catalyst for change, in the running for the highest office in the land.

During her thirty-minute appearance on CBS, Chisholm took the opportunity to admonish the media and media executives directly on the air by calling out how their efforts to ignore her campaign were tantamount to undermining the people's right to vote for their candidate of choice. "The media has no right to determine the frontrunners. The people should get a chance to hear from new segments of the population, not just warmed over candidates..." Translation: The media undermines our democracy and voters' rights when they choose to exclusively cover the candidates who they deem are worthy. She added, "What gives networks the right to ascertain whose candidacy is more important than mine?" The answer, under federal regulations, was nothing, now that the Appellate Court had ruled in Chisholm's favor in 1972.

While a full half hour for uncensored, uninterrupted airtime was beyond many Black media professionals' scope of imagination at the time, the American people still never got the opportunity to witness Chisholm participate in a full-length, in-person presidential primary debate standing opposite her opponents. Even visualizing Chisholm standing onstage behind a large podium going toe to toe with Senator McGovern and Senator Humphrey, amplifying her platform and her policy ideas to women, young people, and Black and brown voters, while questioning her opponents on their own commitments, is exhilarating. Her win against the FCC, ABC, and CBS, though hard-fought and well-earned, ultimately siloed her from the race, creating a perception that her campaign existed outside of the normal election cycle, rather than right at its center.

In 1972, the editorial decisions in newsrooms and networks across the nation left gaping holes in the presidential primary campaign. From headlines and segments that mocked the first Black presidential primary candidate, to the absence of coverage of her campaign entirely, these misses were what informed the public's perceptions about who was capable of running worthy, relevant campaigns for president. From one news story to the next, the media perpetuated the notion that it was better to continue betting on the wealthy white men with a centuries-long stronghold on leadership and a track record of dismissing the people's needs than take a chance on a candidate who sought to break down barriers and set a new plane of political possibilities for our nation. It wasn't the coverage voters deserved then, and a lot of the same gaps still puncture our media landscape today. Unfortunately, this reality leaves the onus on individuals to seek information beyond what's presented to them in daily broadcasts, newspaper headlines, and social media "clickbait."

To fill this void, the field of journalism has expanded and forged platforms to share stories and perspectives from marginalized communities. Black-focused media outlets founded in the late 1940s and the 1950s, such as *Ebony* and *Jet* magazine, created an on-ramp for *Essence* in the 1970s, and *TheGrio* in 2009. Nonprofit platforms such as *ProPublica* now take on investigative reporting to expose the truth about leaders and national institutions. Feminist interests remain at the core of *Ms.* magazine, which was launched as an insert in *New York Magazine* in 1971. And The 19th* News leveraged a nonprofit model to explore gender and politics when it was founded in 2020. Their name is a reference to the Nineteenth Amendment of the US Constitution, which "made voting a right regardless of gender" in 1920, and the asterisk recognizes that it took four more decades before Black and brown women gained the right to vote. In addition, young independent journalists and content creators are taking on the responsibility of sharing relevant, accessible, factual information with their communities through social media as more traditional media outlets, such as newspapers and cable news, fade away. These creators and outlets have expanded on David Frost's original mission of sharing the truth through human-centered stories and highlighting communities that have been traditionally marginalized. In doing so, they are granting their readers and viewers access and sharing their perspectives in a way that fosters community.

These modern outlets were created from necessity for better representation and independence. And they now wield the same power that Shirley Chisholm fought for as she rightfully questioned and challenged the media in 1972. In a precarious moment defined by extremely low public trust in the media, curiosity and a hunger for knowledge are imperative for our humanity and collective survival. In the realm of politics, that means reviewing stories across multiple media sources to compare coverage, identifying discrepancies, and understanding which perspectives are being omitted—and where to find them yourself. It means attending forums in one's community to engage with candidates to assess their abilities beyond what's framed in the media. And it means amplifying the truth repeatedly, for the sake of us all.

CHAPTER SIX

THE CELEBRITY INFLUENCE

"My activism has always existed. My art gave me the platform to do something..."

—Harry Belafonte, "The Scotsman Interview"

By 1972, Motown Records founder Berry Gordy was no stranger to Beverly Hills. Two years prior, the music mogul decided to fully relocate Motown's headquarters from Detroit, Michigan, to Los Angeles, California—a decision for which he was widely criticized back in the Motor City. Detroit had become deeply connected with Motown, culturally and financially. Born from an $800 investment from Gordy's family and modeled after a car factory assembly line, Motown and Detroit had become synonymous for their authentic roots, beautiful melodies, stunning Black talent, and local economic impact. Through the years, Gordy had purchased multiple homes and buildings in the city for Motown's Hitsville USA operations. He hired people from the local neighborhoods as receptionists and assistants, and he nurtured homegrown singers and performers who reign as household names. So, uprooting the business from Detroit felt like a betrayal for many, especially in the largely Black and low-income community where Gordy established the company. Even so, the move to Tinseltown catapulted Gordy into a spot among the stars. In fact, Gordy's neighbor in Beverly Hills was none other than Diahann Carroll.

Just a few months before the Welcome to Hollywood party, Gordy purchased a new home in Bel Air, selling his previous Hollywood home to Diahann Carroll's ex-husband, Monte Kay. As Hollywood connections often go, Gordy's and Carroll's lives and social circles were well intertwined. So it was only right that when Gordy made his way into Carroll's mansion for the party, he immediately wrapped her in a bear hug and laid a giant kiss on her cheek. Carroll, not missing a beat, laughingly returned his embrace in a moment captured by the party photographer. How else would you greet a friend of more than ten years? Their comfort and playfulness had been instant from the moment they met following the US premiere of Carroll's hit play, *No*

Strings, at the Fisher Theater in Detroit in February 1962. After Carroll gave a Tony Award–winning performance as the lead actress of the production, Gordy waited backstage after the show to introduce himself. He was enamored with Carroll's grace, and it's safe to say that Carroll was Gordy's type—slender, stunning, and with a sensational stage presence—the type of talent, that is, that he was developing at Motown. Around the same time, Gordy was crafting the sound and image of none other than Diana Ross and The Supremes.

Carroll considered Gordy to be a genius for the way he built Motown from the ground up, and how his resounding success matched his lasting cultural impact. As doo-wop faded away as the preeminent genre on the airwaves, Gordy ushered in the sounds of soul and R&B music, leading Motown to redefine global music industry norms. Carroll sought to leverage her and Gordy's celebrity and cultural influence in this historic political moment to reach voters who were also fans of Gordy's company and his big-name acts. And it made sense that she would insist on his presence at an event honoring a fellow cultural phenom—Shirley Chisholm.

Interestingly enough, a lot of Gordy's business principles were in direct contrast with what Chisholm stood for. To understand the divergence of thought, and practice, between the Motown legend and the presidential candidate, it's important to understand how Berry Gordy came into power. Motown Records provided the world's soundtrack for life in the '60s and '70s, and Berry Gordy hand-selected nearly every single song. There were hits like the silky smooth "My Girl," by The Temptations, which drove crowds crazy as David Ruffin made his debut in the group. The song also garnered the group their first No. 1 hit on the *Billboard* Hot 100 list. Then there was the bold love declaration "Stop! In the Name of Love," by the most glamorous act on Motown's roster, The Supremes. Through the ladies' elegant choreography, their sleek, high-fashion gowns, and Diana Ross' signature breathy voice, this song became synonymous with the group. There was the genius of "Little Stevie Wonder" in "Fingertips," a song he improvised live onstage at the Apollo Theatre in 1962 at the tender age of twelve years old. Instead of taking his bow, Wonder asked the crowd to clap their hands "just a little bit louder," and a new No. 1 hit emerged organically. And among Motown's hundreds of clever, catchy hits, there was also the abundantly peppy "ABC" by the Jackson 5, which knocked "Let it Be," the latest song from the Beatles, the biggest British band in history, out of the top spot on the Billboard Hot 100 list in January 1970.

These songs represent the quality of product Motown released. Moreover, they marked the rise of Black cultural influence in America. As the civil rights movement gained national momentum, Gordy developed acts that had crossover and mass media appeal as segregationist policies began to fall across the nation. As a businessman, Gordy developed each record with his legendary quality control process, which featured open dialogue during a weekly product evaluation meeting. There were only three rules when it came to the quality control meetings: "1) No Producer could vote for his own record [to be released to record stores and radio stations]; 2) Only [Gordy] could overrule a majority vote; and 3) Anyone more than 5 minutes late [to the meeting] would be locked out [of the conference room]." If there were ever any split decisions, Gordy would ask one quintessential question that clarified fans' priorities: "If you had one dollar and you were hungry, would you buy this record or a hot dog?" With this question, Gordy centered Black fans in the Detroit neighborhood who had limited resources from their low-wage jobs, even as Motown enjoyed support from white Americans who were so intoxicated by Motown's sound that race wasn't a barrier to buying the records of Black artists.

Anything short of an immediate response of "buy the record" made its way to the scraps.

The signature Motown sound was all about fun, rhythm, and an infectious lightness that sugarcoated even the most heartbreaking lyrics with joy, likely a subtle analogy for the Black experience in America. Consider The Supremes' first No. 1 hit, "Where Did Our Love Go," which was released in 1964, the same year that Congress passed the Civil Rights Act. In the midst of the nation's attempt to codify the anti-discrimination act, "Where Did Our Love Go," flooded the airwaves with happy claps and light chimes. The energy of the song flows quickly as the piano chords bounce over the clapped rhythm, leaving listeners minimal space to absorb Diana Ross' perfectly enunciated pleas for her boyfriend not to leave her all by herself. All the while, listeners would shimmy to the beat, ignoring Ross' desperation and pain. The Supremes recorded the music video in Paris, France, where they danced through traffic and playfully smiled at the cameras and passersby. The video ends abruptly with a white police officer pushing the group out of the street, even grabbing one of the singers to physically move her onto the sidewalk. That physical action was yet another reminder of how Black people, no matter how famous or how visually vibrant and jubilant, could easily have their autonomy and their joy snatched away at a moment's notice. And the way the singers continued to smile as they were being harassed by the officers represented how Black people are so often expected to smile and perform through the daily pains of injustice, targeted violence, and racism. In the 1960s, that included being rejected from lunch counters, being attacked by police when attempting to vote, and being forced to attend subpar schools without resources. This music represented a reprieve for Black audiences, while still entertaining them *and* the masses. This duality—of creating joy for Black people while also ensuring that white people were sufficiently entertained—was central to Motown's success.

The Motown sound was magical, the sound was alluring, and the sound produced a formula that yielded massive hits for Gordy. Hits so big that the Beatles even requested permission to cover, record, and release versions of "Money (That's What I Want)" by Barrett Strong, and "Please Mr. Postman," by the Marvelettes, on their early albums. Black influence was essential to the formula that propelled Motown to become the biggest Black-owned business in the nation in the 1960s. Black artists, Black entrepreneurs, Black sound was their model, just as it continues to be the model for some of the biggest non-Black acts who co-opt original Black sounds today.

Gordy had a moneymaking machine that operated with the efficiency of an assembly line. Any disruptions to the line, or to the product's crossover appeal, would not be tolerated. That sentiment was captured in the strict artist contracts, the boundaries set on artists' personal lives, and the training and etiquette courses artists were required to take. For example, when Stevie Wonder signed a contract with Motown at just eleven years old, he was given an allowance of only $200 per month, and the rest of his earnings were put into a trust that was managed by Motown, to which Wonder's mother objected but ultimately relented. There were grueling artist development classes that were meant to refine Motown groups before public appearances and performances. To make the cut, acts had to impress vocal coaches, dance instructors, choreographers, stylists, designers, and charm school instructors. Yes, charm school lessons were required, particularly for the women of Motown. From makeup tutorials and posture drills to manners and image management, Maxine Powell of the Maxine Powell Finishing School enforced strict rules to make sure Motown's stars and starlets were red carpet and interview ready.

Gordy recalled overhearing Powell tell the ladies, "Smoking or drinking in public? Ladies don't do that sort of thing." And when it came to music production, Gordy didn't want his artists to deviate from their finely developed formula.

However, as political and social issues gripped the nation in the late 1960s and early 1970s, there were Motown artists who wanted to make direct declarations about their stances and beliefs related to the struggles of the times and of their people. One of the era's most notorious musical showdowns about public political statements featured Marvin Gaye and his famous 1971 protest song, "What's Going On," and album with the same name. At the time that Gaye began developing the album, the Vietnam War was raging with no end in sight and expanding into Cambodia. The nation was still reeling from the Ohio National Guard shooting anti-war protesters at Kent State University. Police brutality and the systematic targeting of Black people in Detroit was off the charts in the wake of the 1967 Detroit riot, which saw tanks rolling down residential streets. The world was a pressure cooker of outrage and frustration, and Gaye wanted to communicate his own anger and make a statement about the unrest he was witnessing. His own brother, Frankie, returned home from Vietnam and started sharing stories about his experience.

As soon as Gaye told Berry Gordy about his vision for the album, Gordy objected, telling him, "Stick to what works," referring to the signature Motown sound of fluffy love songs, and Gaye's personal brand as a sexy crooner. Up to this point, Gaye's biggest hits were duets with Tammi Terrell, such as "You're All I Need to Get By," and soul-stirring, jilted love songs like "I Heard It Through the Grapevine." In Gordy's mind, Marvin Gaye was set as a lovable playboy, not a socially conscious protest artist. Gordy also added, "If you're going to do something different, at least make it commercial... Marvin, you've got this great, sexy image and you've got to protect it." That comment triggered something in Gaye, and in an interview, he said, "I had to fight for my creative freedom, my artistic freedom, my right to produce, my right to write."

It is unclear why Gaye had to fight Gordy as hard as he did to make a political statement when just one year prior, Motown released multiple political songs. In 1970, Motown released "Ball of Confusion" by The Temptations, a song with lyrics that captured the chaos of the war, rising unemployment, drug use among young people, and disillusionment with the political system. Gordy himself described the song as having electric yet melodic tracks. The song was a hit, reaching No. 3 on the pop charts, and it was followed by "War," by Edwin Starr. "War" defined the Vietnam War as "an enemy to all mankind," and it became a bona fide No. 1 hit on the Billboard Hot 100 list. Perhaps the distinction here is that there was an explicit audience for Gaye's anti-war anthem. By 1970, the Vietnam War was deeply unpopular with the general public as the loss of life was overwhelming, and the government's continual investment in the war was seen as a diversion from domestic issues, such as quality housing and education. That sentiment was also captured in polling in the summer of 1970 that showed that 56 percent of adults believed that the Vietnam War was a mistake, and in mass movements such as the student strike across 900 college campuses in May 1970.

And yet Gordy was adamant that Marvin Gaye's songs about war and police brutality were "taking things too far." Gordy recalled, "I was against him writing about trigger happy police, stuff about the world... war... I said, well, we can't do that." He added, "[Motown artists] have freedom within restriction.... I'm not gonna tell you anything you're going to do between here and here. But when you get past there, I have to stop you." To counter Gordy's adamant position, Marvin Gaye drew a clear red line when he told Motown, "Put it out or I'll never record for you again." Gaye played it masterfully. "What's Going On" became a critically acclaimed hit song and album, and its release signaled his transition toward becoming a socially and politically engaged musical artist. He successfully wielded his celebrity to convey a political message that reflected the times. The titular track called out the senseless deaths of young Black men, how protesters should not be met with brutality, and the public cry that "war is not the answer." Gaye's stunning lyrics, backed by a screaming saxophone, reflected the torment many felt at the time, and their cries and demands for change. "What's Going On" peaked at No. 2 on the Billboard Hot 100 and spent fifty-three weeks on the pop charts. Keeping in mind the intention of this record, and the fight Gaye put up to bring it to listeners in 1971, it's no surprise that he omitted Gordy from the album's acknowledgments. Simply put, Berry Gordy was wrong.

Gordy's entrenched position against Gaye's historic album begs the question: Why did the man who tried to block the best-known protest album in the nation from seeing the light of day attend a fundraiser for a political candidate who endorsed the same anti-war, anti-police brutality agenda that Gaye centered in his music?

Shirley Chisholm had been protesting the war in Vietnam since 1969. She supported protests against police brutality and protests for workers' rights and fair wages. She was a political leader who was committed to flipping American politics on its head—actions Gordy considered "going too far" when it came to the music. The press and her legislative colleagues had long labeled Chisholm a disruptor, or as she more aptly defined herself, a "catalyst for change." Her entire campaign ethos was about taking up the space that was rightfully hers as a citizen, as a woman, and as a Black person. Chisholm did not shrink herself, mince words, or modify her posture to appeal to white people, rich people, or any person with authority. She certainly did not attend anyone's charm school. If anything, she consistently doubled down on her principles to shake harmful systems and the people who perpetuate them in the most productive ways. Everything Chisholm represented was in direct opposition to Berry Gordy's entire business model. Motown developed Black performers through years of training and outfitted them in finery in order to achieve broad crossover appeal among white consumers and the mass media. Surely, their true personalities and beliefs were tamped down in the process—as Gaye experienced until he broke out of the mold.

On the one hand, there is a categorical difference between the commercial viability and entertainment potential of a protest album, and simply attending a party for a political candidate who was more committed to social change than appealing to broad audiences. Gordy didn't have to produce or release a product with his name on it for this fundraiser. It was a private event, and he wasn't even officially endorsing Chisholm. So, attending the Welcome to Hollywood party could be seen as a low-stakes commitment for Gordy compared to the development and release of an album for one of the biggest artists on his record label at the time.

On the other hand, one year after the release and subsequent commercial and critical success of Gaye's album, Gordy was probably a bit more comfortable with direct expressions of protest and political beliefs. Gordy's big fear about Gaye's *What's Going On* album had been that it wouldn't sell because it wasn't Gaye's usual sexy brand, but it sold and charted just as well as other Motown hits. Ever the businessman, Gordy celebrated the album's success at each turn, noting his own surprise at Gaye's growth and artistry as he had written and produced this body of work on his own. He went so far as to admit his error in his memoir stating, "I learned something." He learned that politics can be profitable, especially when it resonates with the national mood and shifting culture. It's reminiscent of that powerful lyric about cash by Wu-Tang.

Either way, Gordy more than likely recognized the strategic benefit of being in the room. Picture him sipping champagne, eating caviar, and mingling around Diahann Carroll's black tile veranda with some of Hollywood's biggest stars, all in the name of supporting a campaign that would go on to leave a lasting impression on American politics. Chisholm's presidential campaign was Black history in real time, and the Welcome to Hollywood party was the sole celebrity event for her campaign in Southern California. FOMO, aka the fear of missing out, was likely another factor in his calculus for attending. That, plus the fact that when Diahann Carroll tells you to come to her mansion for an event, you show up!

Carroll was consistent and vocal about her support for Shirley Chisholm, and she built a guest list that rivaled red carpets. In the weeks leading up to the party, not only did she sing onstage at a Chisholm rally in New York, but she had also been promoting the Welcome to Hollywood party in the press, garnering coverage in the social sections of newspapers on both coasts. Her quotes in the *LA Times*, for example, emphasized how she believed Chisholm had something to offer this nation. Carroll's name in print as a Shirley Chisholm supporter sent a signal to the newspaper's more than 1 million daily readers that made them sit up and pay just a little more attention to Shirley Chisholm. This was their favorite on-screen nurse publicly inviting her fans—who had purchased *Julia* lunch boxes and Mattel's *Julia* doll dressed in a nurse's uniform for their children—to take a look at Chisholm. This was the glamorous singer, and Broadway performer whom they adored telling the public that Chisholm's ideas were worthy of their attention and their vote. Carroll was calling them in, just like she did with her invitation to Berry Gordy.

Whether she knew it or not, Carroll was a celebrity surrogate for a cutting-edge candidate. Through her media engagements, she drummed up positive press coverage and public attention for Chisholm, whose candidacy had been largely dismissed. By engaging her own network to attend the Welcome to Hollywood fundraiser, Carroll was casting a wide net to increase Chisholm's reach and support. And by opening her home to co-host the fundraiser with Flip Wilson, and by performing at Chisholm events in New York, Carroll was adding much-needed financial resources to the campaign. When it came to representing the campaign as an external voice and celebrity supporter, she was the total package.

By lending her fame, her time, and her home to the Chisholm campaign during the Democratic presidential primary election, Carroll set a model for campaign surrogates that we still see used today. In 2012, Kerry Washington, or as we affectionately call her in the Black community, "Olivia Pope," strutted onto the scene as lead character on the primetime network drama *Scandal.* Like Carroll, Washington broke through cultural barriers to become a Black woman starring in her own hit network television show, this time more than forty years after *Julia* had premiered. Both women have their fingerprints all over Hollywood and the entertainment industry. With their lead roles, they both challenged and reset notions about what a Black woman looked like and how she behaved on-screen. For Washington, *Scandal* brought to life a multidimensional character whose personal life was a mess while her professional life flourished—a notion that many professional women, especially Black women, who are denied the space for imperfection, understand deeply. Seeing Washington as a lead Black character who wielded authority in the notoriously white, elite, wealthy world of politics, was something that gave viewers and Black staffers in Washington, DC, particular delight. Creator Shonda Rhimes' layered storytelling behind Olivia Pope's personal journey highlighted challenges to socially acceptable white supremacist norms. Consider the Season 3 premiere episode, "It's Handled," which featured an exchange between the fictional Olivia Pope and her father, Rowan Pope, portrayed masterfully by Joe Morton. Rowan confronts Olivia about the need to be twice as good as white people to achieve half as much as they are easily afforded. It was canon. Black viewers understood the concept deeply because many had heard that phrase from a parent or an elder at least once in their lives. Comparatively, non-Black viewers got a glimpse of the pressures and unrealistic standards that Black people experience while operating in predominantly white sectors, like politics.

Similar to Chisholm's effect on Carroll's political sensibilities, Kerry Washington was also inspired by a vibrant, dynamic candidate who was looking to break through barriers to political engagement: Barack Obama. The 2008 Democratic presidential primary election was a contentious series of events. Cultural shifts in politics and digital media were ushering in a new era, and many Democrats presumed that then-Senator Hillary Clinton had the Democratic nomination for the presidency in the bag. Those Democrats would receive a rude awakening when Barack Obama jumped into the race in February 2007, mere weeks after Clinton kicked off her campaign. Pair that fissure with the way that Facebook, the four-year-old social media platform, was driving global connections and conversations on the internet in a new, visual medium. Facebook had an online organizing feature that Obama's campaign team leveraged better than any other candidate at the start of the digital age to tap into small-dollar donations. Grassroots fundraising was officially online, and Obama's supporters were breaking records for his historic campaign. The American people were ready for new energy and fresh ideas after eight years of George W. Bush, multiple wars in the Middle East, and legacy family names running the nation (Hillary Clinton's own bid for the presidency was disproportionately impacted by her husband's extramarital activities and an impeachment that had occurred a decade prior). Nothing in the 2008 presidential election cycle was newer than a young Black man running for the highest office in the land on a platform full of hopeful language and impatient ideas about how to withdraw US troops from Iraq, increase access to quality health care, and make more investments in renewable energy.

As Obama began introducing himself to voters in 2007, early polls showed that he lagged behind Clinton in support by 26 points. But by January 2008, Obama flipped that deficit as polls showed that he led Clinton by 28 points. So what changed? It's an indisputable fact that Obama was, and still is, a charismatic, compelling orator and leader who continues to be one of the most popular Democrats in the nation. And his winning personality, paired with his empowering vision that "one voice could change a nation," made voters feel like he was speaking to them. But the key here was the Obama campaign's brilliant use of celebrity surrogates. These highly famous, and highly likable, individuals joined him on the campaign trail and invited in their networks of fans and friends to take a closer look at the "skinny kid with a funny name," as Obama described himself during his 2004 televised speech at the Democratic National Convention, which served as his national debut.

One celebrity who had a swift and decisive impact was the one and only Oprah Winfrey. Oprah entered the race with an early, ringing endorsement for Obama that went out to her highly engaged television audience. And what's most special about Oprah's audience is that, through the years, they have been primed to respond to her calls to action. Many of Oprah's public declarations and recommendations—from her book club to her annual favorite things gift list—come as trusted recommendations for her devoted fan base. The daytime television queen's endorsement supplemented the Obama campaign's digital activity on Facebook, amplifying his image and message online and promoting his local organizing efforts. Events popped up in communities across the nation as campaign organizers translated voters' excited energy online into in-person phone banks and door-knocking activities. Oprah was the perfect surrogate, especially with the introduction of digital campaigning, because her audience followed her support for Obama from television to social media, and then to the ballot box.

Kerry Washington was also one of Obama's highly engaged celebrity supporters, and for Washington, Obama was her choice from the start. Like many people, Washington was drawn to Obama after his rousing speech at the 2004 Democratic Convention, but she decided to support the campaign after attending the January 2008 primary debate in South Carolina between Obama, Clinton, and former Senator John Edwards. Obama's vision for what the nation could achieve was so infectious that Washington spent that year on and off the campaign trail speaking at campaign fundraisers and rallies. In her memoir, *Thicker Than Water*, she wrote, "What I saw in those sixteen states, many of which I'd never visited before, were people from different backgrounds all yearning for a country with more justice and equity and possibility for everyone. I saw people falling in love with Obama's vision for a truly united country where regardless of race, ethnicity, religion, sexual orientation, physical ability, or socioeconomic background, our humanity is valued and our voices matter." That human-centered appeal and Obama's appreciation for the power of a single voice are what Washington was able to amplify in speeches and events across the nation, further expanding the campaign's reach.

Each time one of Obama's campaign surrogates spoke on his behalf, they were acting as an extension of him and his campaign's vision, and that contributed to his historic election in November 2008. Similar to Diahann Carroll and Shirley Chisholm, celebrity was used in the campaign to amplify a message and reach voters who otherwise weren't engaged in politics or were turned off by the way previous leaders had failed them.

As celebrities and entertainers continue to play an outsized role in culture and politics today, they have the constant ear and attention of prospective voters, and often before political candidates are able to fully communicate their vision for the nation. Similar to Berry Gordy's cultural influence with his slate of celebrity artists at Motown, fans of music, television, and pop culture absorb what their industry favorites say, do, and endorse. In fact, a January 2024 *Newsweek* poll of 1,500 eligible voters showed that 18 percent of respondents would be more likely to support a candidate that Taylor Swift endorses in the 2024 presidential election. While a celebrity's endorsement is no guarantee for a campaign to see an influx of support from voters, what this phenomenon does emphasize is the material impact celebrities can have, especially in elections where the margins for victory will be small. Swift herself is acutely aware that her words and influence prompt action, or inaction, from fans. In her documentary, *Miss Americana*, as Swift was preparing to endorse two Democratic candidates in Tennessee in 2018, her father asked whether she was concerned about news outlets printing, "Taylor Swift comes out against Trump." Without hesitation, Swift responded, "I don't care if they write that. I'm sad that I didn't [denounce Trump] two years ago, but I can't change that."

Unfortunately, there has been a decline in the quality, value, and returns of celebrity endorsements and campaign support. One former campaign staffer who was hired to coordinate celebrity surrogate activities for the 2022 midterm election cycle shared that sometimes celebrities cost the campaigns more than they deliver, as they invoice campaigns for performances and travel accommodations for their management teams. On top of that, oftentimes the "celebrities struggle to communicate even the most basic policy ideas included in the candidate's platform." So instead of raising funds for campaigns, they cost the campaigns money. Instead of amplifying candidates and engaging voters on social media, they don't follow through on public statements of support. And instead of being personally drawn to a candidate's platform, there is minimal personal connection to campaign ideas.

The interactions have become transactional and uninspiring due to the lack of genuine ties to the campaigns, and the high turnover rate of social media virality. While Diahann Carroll felt a direct connection to Shirley Chisholm's platform and her historic campaign, and Kerry Washington was so inspired by President Obama that she extended her work into amplifying state legislative races and voting rights initiatives, that heft and substantive engagement are limited among many celebrities today. And this decline mirrors the increasing disillusion with politics. According to a Pew Research poll during the 2024 primary election, 65 percent of Americans said that they felt exhausted when thinking about politics. When these feelings are paired with the reality that social media is built on the attention economy, this decline appears to be on track. Voters are growing more disengaged with politics out of frustration, and thus they are more willing to look to their preferred celebrities for guidance, when and if they speak out. And a majority of celebrities, who are our culture bearers, have made their endorsements a popularity contest instead of urging people to inform themselves on who's on the ballot.

To make matters worse, celebrity culture has given way to harmful and misinformed political statements. Consider St. Louis rapper Sexyy Red. She is beloved for her unfiltered style of rap; her authentic, relatable personality; and her references to the early 2000s' clothes, dance trends, and culture. Her songs feature playful, infectious lyrics, and her fans connect to her brand of confidence. However, when it comes to politics, her statements are inaccurate. For example, during an interview in late 2023, Sexyy Red declared that Black people "support Trump in the hood." She added, "...Once he started getting Black people out of jail and started giving out that free money, oh we love Trump. We need him back in office." Now, there is no basis of fact for Black people supporting Trump, as only 8 percent of Black people voted for Trump in 2020, and only 6 percent of Black people voted for him in 2016. And when it comes to getting Black people out of jail, Trump granted only 237 acts of clemency, compared to 1,927 acts of clemency by Barack Obama. And yet during the Super Bowl, a program that charges advertisers millions of dollars for a single ad spot, Trump's campaign ran an ad featuring Alice Marie Johnson, a sixty-three-year-old woman whose life sentence Trump commuted. And just days before the 2020 election, pictures of Lil Wayne with Trump giving a thumbs-up circulated after the beloved rapper received a presidential pardon. And as for those stimulus checks, it was Democrats in Congress who pushed for citizens to receive multiple direct payments throughout the pandemic, while Republicans overwhelmingly opposed those measures in fear of a pandemic-induced economic freefall. But since Trump made the unprecedented move to put his name on the relief checks, he wrongly gets the credit.

There's also the jarring experience of watching New York rapper Fat Joe declaring that he had to get his hands on a pair of golden Trump-branded sneakers, and promoting them online while simultaneously stating that he is not a Trumper and would never vote for him. The shoe is called the "Never Surrender High-Tops," a reference to the January 6, 2021, insurrection. Trump made the unplanned announcement, unveiling the sneaker at Sneaker Con in Philadelphia just one day after a judge ordered him to pay a $355 million penalty for fraudulent business practices, inflating his wealth on financial statements, and deceiving banks and insurers in New York.

The campaign's move was particularly sinister as sneaker culture is deeply embedded within Black and brown communities. The shoe costs $399, and Trump's campaign hoped that the sneakers would attract more young voters and voters of color. (Trump maintains that his appeal to Black and brown voters is connected to his felony charges and his mug shot.) Cue Fat Joe's social media live stream. Simply put, his actions sent mixed signals to the hundreds of thousands of people who watched online.

Fat Joe's live stream, Berry Gordy's opposition to the *What's Going On* album, and the voters who will vote for whomever Taylor Swift tells them to, begs the questions: Where are the boundaries for celebrity influence and power? What are the limits for cultural influence in a social-media-led landscape where we never really log off the internet? Is the limit determined when a person's right to vote is suppressed to the point that standing in hours-long lines is the norm on Election Day? Is the limit established when people realize that they don't actually have a fair shot to make a livable wage, much less equal wages with their more privileged peers, in this economic system?

Shirley Chisholm believed that celebrity and cultural influence is bound by people standing in their individual autonomy and discernment. The same autonomy that she declared with each of her political actions—be it running for president, opposing the Vietnam War, or telling a young student that registering to vote is the first step to supporting her mission. She was resolute in her commitment to thinking for herself, and helping others do the same by modeling her discernment and challenging them in real time. Consider it her version of tough love, similar to her conversation with a young Barbara Lee.

Each individual has an opportunity to reframe their perspective and how they engage with celebrity culture in their daily lives and their political decisions. It starts with self-awareness and a keen eye on one's own needs and their community's needs. It extends to demanding solutions to address the issues no matter what your "faves" in the industry are doing, or not doing, for that matter. Marvin Gaye stepped into this vulnerable position when he insisted on producing and releasing the *What's Going On* album in spite of Gordy's objections. And through his actions, Gaye effectively challenged Gordy, someone he respected, in order to deliver a critical political message to the masses via his musical artistry. That's where the individual's power lies.

CHAPTER SEVEN

THE (WHITE) FEMINISTS

"We knew that there could be no real sisterhood between white women and women of color if white women were not able to divest of white supremacy..."

—bell hooks, *Feminism Is for Everybody: Passionate Politics*

Hollywood's blonde bombshell and funny girl of the late 1960s, Goldie Hawn, flitted carefree through the crowd at the Welcome to Hollywood fundraiser. The media had dubbed her the "elusive butterfly," thanks to her forthcoming film, *Butterflies Are Free*, and the fact that she arrived at Diahann Carroll's home without her husband. It's doubtful that any of the other attendees at the party noticed, or cared, that Hawn attended the party alone, but they likely wondered about her presence at an event to honor Shirley Chisholm and raise money for her presidential run.

Though she'd been in Hollywood for only about six years after working as a professional go-go dancer in New York, Goldie Hawn's career had taken off like a bottle rocket. In 1968, with her giggling ditzy girl comedic style, Hawn transitioned from a go-go dancer to a weekly player on the NBC sketch comedy series *Laugh-In*, where appearing in a bikini with body paint and flubbing her lines was all part of her appeal to the show's 50 million weekly viewers. Hawn was also a surprise winner at the 1970 Academy Awards for her supporting role in the film adaptation of the Broadway production *Cactus Flower*. Her performance in this film caught critics off guard, as they were prepared to dismiss her as merely a fine specimen to observe, instead of the multidimensional performer she was becoming. Between American film critic Roger Ebert writing, "Wow!—Goldie Hawn," and a reviewer for the *New York Times* declaring, "... it comes as a pleasing jolt to find the youngster, Goldie Hawn, at the apex of the triangle, not only beautifully holding her own with the two veteran stars but also enhancing the content and flavor of the movie," Hawn forged her place as a Hollywood A-lister.

Hawn's career was on a continuous upward trajectory, something that even she did not internalize fully in the late 1960s. She was famously absent from the 1970 Academy Awards ceremony. In fact, she'd forgotten that the award show was airing! Fred Astaire announced that she'd won the Oscar for Best Supporting Actress at the ceremony while Hawn was asleep in London. She received a phone call in the middle of the night and found out she won, and she later expressed regret about not attending the ceremony. "I never got dressed up. I never got to pick up the award... I regret it. It's something that I look back on now and think, 'It would have been so great to be able to have done that.'" It's understandable that a twenty-four-year-old wouldn't want to get her hopes up about winning an Oscar for her very first film role, especially while up against established actresses like Dyan Cannon in *Bob & Carol & Ted & Alice*, and Sylvia Miles in *Midnight Cowboy*. A win for Hawn felt completely implausible, and yet her performance was deemed *that* good.

Despite cutting through the noise, there was still outspoken dissent about how Hawn portrayed herself on-screen. As the women's liberation movement gained momentum in the late 1960s and early 1970s, Hawn found herself in the crosshairs of feminist ideals when a journalist at a women's magazine questioned her about making it big by playing a stereotypical blonde. "She said to me, 'Well, don't you feel kind of irresponsible for being like a dumb blonde and, you know, playing dumb in a time when women are reaching out to become independent and liberated,'... And I looked at her and I said, 'Oh, but I'm already liberated.'" In Goldie Hawn's eyes, she was a liberated woman, and a feminist—even if some feminists didn't understand that she was living the very principles that they were protesting for in real time. Moreover, Hawn's interaction with the journalist reflected the fissures within the feminist movement. By the late 1960s, Black women had called out feminist leaders for prioritizing the needs of middle-class white women over those of Black women. Lesbians and queer women pushed for equal rights and protections, and to be acknowledged alongside gay men as their parallel struggle gained traction. Competing definitions of feminism emerged. As Hawn pointed out to the journalist, there was no one way to be a feminist. Rather, by choosing her roles, honing her comedic skills, and not shrinking or changing course when criticized, Hawn was exercising her autonomy as a woman, which is an underlying principle of feminism that has since been practiced by other famous blondes, namely Dolly Parton and Madonna.

It's not as though Hawn was deeply entrenched in the feminist movement, especially with the level of condemnation that she was receiving from other women. Still, she had a firm sense of what she wanted and how she could achieve it, no matter the obstacles. Elaborating on her interaction with the journalist years later, Hawn noted that she believes liberation comes in two tiers—externally from social standards and expectations, which the journalist had explicitly attempted to force on her, and internally from one's inner voice. "My sense of liberation and the freedom to speak the way I want to and to feel solid in my shoes was getting stronger and stronger. That's what helps me move through other people's perceptions of how I should or should not be liberated. I would never listen to those rules." Rejecting the rules was the entire point of the women's liberation movement, and Hawn knew the extent of her personal power, even if the public didn't understand it early in her career.

By the time of the Welcome to Hollywood party, Hawn was a star who warranted an invitation to exclusive events. She could have easily been invited by our host herself, Diahann Carroll, with whom she shared mutual friends in the industry, such as legendary singer and performer Sammy Davis Jr. But no matter who invited her, one glaring question was how Hawn could square her attendance at the Shirley Chisholm fundraiser with her visible, consistent support for Chisholm's Democratic primary opponent, Senator George McGovern.

According to the media coverage, almost every time McGovern was in California for events to raise funds for his campaign, Goldie Hawn was there to lend her celebrity and her wallet to his cause. There was the McGovern fundraiser dinner at the Beverly Wilshire's ballroom, where supporters dined with the stars. The concert fundraiser at the Forum, where Hawn served as an usher alongside Jack Nicholson, Gene Hackman, and James Earl Jones just days before the Shirley Chisholm party. There was the San Francisco Rock and Roll Benefit, where Hawn engaged with McGovern supporters. Hawn was also publicly listed as a McGovern campaign donor in the first quarter fundraising reports. Hawn appeared to be all in on McGovern. She went so far as to declare to the press, "[McGovern] is the only light I see for America...I think McGovern understands that the young people are the future of this country, and I think when he's president he'll act to see that this country has a future."

One could surmise that Goldie Hawn attended the Welcome to Hollywood fundraiser for similar reasons as Berry Gordy: history was being made and she didn't want to miss out. Hawn, as a liberated woman herself, may have also been motivated to demonstrate a degree of public awareness and acknowledgment of the first woman making a substantive run for the Democratic nomination for the presidency. Even taking a brief moment to mingle with supporters of Chisholm from all corners of the entertainment industry was a sign of respect, but it most certainly was not what Chisholm wanted from liberated, feminist white women. Hawn was hedging—limiting her support for Chisholm to this visible Hollywood event while maintaining her support for a different, white male candidate. And that noncommittal position had, and continues to have, political and social consequences.

From the beginning, Chisholm communicated directly to feminist leaders and organizers that if they were going to stand with her, then she only wanted their full, sustained support. During a regional convening for the National Organization for Women (NOW), a feminist organization committed to gaining equal human rights for all women, Chisholm told conference attendees, "I don't want half-baked endorsements, I want wholehearted people... If you're going to be with me in a half-hearted fashion, don't come with me at all." It was a simple, reasonable request. Chisholm's definition of the buy-in that she wanted from women's groups was rooted in her knowledge of how their support could legitimize her campaign. Anyone who endorsed her would serve as a validator to the press and to other established politicians, who repeatedly asked: Is Shirley Chisholm a serious candidate or not?

While Chisholm's endorsement request appeared to be simple enough, only a few of her closest feminist allies delivered. The Black and Latina founders of the National Women's Political Caucus (NWPC), a nonpartisan, multicultural grassroots organization dedicated to increasing women's political participation, proved more than ready to answer Chisholm's call for unequivocal support. Initial support for Chisholm also came from political powerhouses such as Fannie Lou Hamer, a Black voting rights and reproductive rights activist from Mississippi. Hamer had famously challenged the Democratic Party to recognize the Mississippi Freedom Democratic Party delegation in a nationally covered speech during the 1964 convention. Martin Luther King Jr. noted that Hamer's testimony before the convention's credentials committee "educated a nation and brought the political powers to their knees in repentance." Throughout the campaign, Hamer expressed her pride in supporting Chisholm, and after casting her ballot at the Democratic Convention, she declared, "Chisholm talked about 'the real issues in the country' that the male candidates had not talked about, and refused to 'bow to political pressure.'"

Another early feminist supporter was Lupe Anguiano, a Mexican American nun who became a political activist after an archbishop directed her to stop protesting against discriminatory housing policies. Anguiano's activism also included organizing the Michigan grape boycott of 1965 alongside Cesar Chavez, and advising presidents on bilingual education and welfare reform policies. Anguiano understood the importance of her early endorsement as Chisholm's campaign was always about setting the table for future political gains for women of color. Chisholm also enjoyed the support of Gwendolyn Cherry, the first Black woman to practice law in Dade County, Florida, and the first African American woman to be elected to the Florida legislature. Cherry also didn't hesitate to support the first Black woman seeking the Democratic nomination. And not only did she endorse Chisholm, but she also called out the Congressional Black Caucus for attempting to exclude Chisholm from speaking on a panel related to organizing for the future. In the middle of the discussions, Cherry asked, "[Why is] our presidential candidate not here?" After which Shirley Chisholm stood and walked to the microphone to address the crowd. These feminist activists of color knew what it meant to fight to take up space that was rightfully theirs, and they were willing to join Chisholm in her endeavor to redefine political possibilities.

Their support stood in direct contrast with white feminist leaders of the time. One of Chisholm's earliest supporters, Betty Friedan, author of *The Feminine Mystique*, co-founder of the National

Organization for Women, and co-founder of the National Women's Political Caucus (NWPC), had encouraged Chisholm to run for president as early as mid-1971 so that she could announce her campaign in August 1971 on Women's Equality Day. Unfortunately, as soon as Senator Gene McCarthy announced his 1972 campaign for president, Friedan split her loyalties. She promised Chisholm that she would support her campaign while she would also campaign for McCarthy in states where he was on the ballot and Chisholm was not. Representative Bella Abzug, one of Chisholm's New York counterparts in Congress and another co-founder of NWPC, also chose to offer Chisholm limited support. Abzug requested to join Chisholm at her Washington press conference immediately following her official campaign announcement. During the press conference, Representatives Ron Dellums of California and Parren Mitchell of Maryland, both members of the Congressional Black Caucus, endorsed Chisholm and expressed their full support for her presidential bid. When Abzug addressed the crowd, she welcomed Chisholm's candidacy for the presidency, but did not explicitly endorse her campaign, citing her commitment to the nonpartisan National Women's Political Caucus. Considering that the NWPC was created with the goal of increasing women's political engagement, it would have been fully aligned with their mission to endorse Chisholm, the lone woman candidate. Even Chisholm expressed surprise toward this move from Abzug, writing in her memoir, *The Good Fight*, "It was a letdown. It was also bewildering: if she intended to sit on the fence, why did she ask to appear with me at my announcement for the Presidency?" The fear of missing out on a historic moment, or not being visible in the midst of a feminist feat, appears to have been at least a partial motivation for Abzug. Ultimately, Abzug wouldn't endorse Chisholm at any point during the primary, though she offered complimentary public comments during events, including describing a dream cabinet for President Shirley Chisholm during a convening.

Just as Abzug and Friedan refused to exclusively endorse Shirley Chisholm's candidacy, renowned women's liberation leader Gloria Steinem followed suit. Steinem had essentially served as the face of the feminist movement starting in the 1960s, after she made national news by reporting as an undercover Playboy Bunny at the New York City Playboy Club, and covering issues including access to contraception and abortion for *Esquire* and *New York Magazine*. Her exposé, "A Bunny's Tale," painted a dark portrait of the sexism and sexual harassment that young women faced at the club, and was a precursor to her own media projects dedicated to highlighting the stories and the demands of women, like *Ms.* magazine. In addition to her journalism, Steinem was also a co-founder of the National Women's Political Caucus. In spite of her feminist dedication, when it came to Chisholm's presidential run, Steinem declared in public statements and press interviews that she supported Chisholm's candidacy, but she believed that George McGovern was the "best white male candidate" in the race. She also declared that there was no conflict in supporting both Chisholm and McGovern because she, too, would only campaign for McGovern in states where Chisholm was not on the ballot. Steinem contorted herself in an effort to thread this needle, though her previous support for McGovern during the 1968 presidential election cycle, during which she brought in one of McGovern's biggest donors, foreshadowed her choice to "sit on the fence."

Ultimately, Steinem's efforts to split her support were insufficient, as it signaled to the public that there must be a reason why she wasn't all in on Chisholm's candidacy. For all of her feminist positions, she still felt the need to turn to a man to realize political goals that directly affected women. The decision to hedge was in direct conflict with her work at NWPC, and with her identity as a feminist, especially as Steinem openly recognized that McGovern's campaign merely positioned its women staffers as superficial props versus advisors and decision makers. Meanwhile, the Chisholm campaign was the direct opposite to McGovern's when it came to women staffers. Women were empowered under Chisholm's leadership on the campaign trail and in Congress. They worked as trusted advisors and ran her offices in a semi-autonomous fashion. There was no question about which candidate valued women and prioritized policies related to women, but still, Steinem, Friedan, Abzug, and Goldie Hawn could dare to stand only at the edges of Chisholm's feminist bid for the presidency.

Steinem's hedging came to a boiling point in early 1972 when she and Chisholm appeared for a joint interview on the Chicago WLS-TV program *Kennedy and Company*. Steinem was energetic in the interview, describing how she and Chisholm corresponded via telegram on the campaign trail, and how she was dividing her support between Chisholm and McGovern. Hearing Steinem describe her split loyalty on camera got under Chisholm's skin, and photographs of the conversation reveal a level of rigidity in Chisholm's posture as Steinem spoke. While this wasn't the first time Chisholm witnessed noncommittal support by one of her close allies, it was the last straw, as it happened on live television. After the interview, Chisholm told Steinem, "Gloria, you're supporting either George McGovern or Shirley Chisholm. I don't mind if you are supporting George. If he is your candidate, so be it, but don't do me any favors by giving me this semi-endorsement. I don't need that kind of help." Chisholm's demand for Steinem to choose a singular side was rooted in the reality that, oftentimes, white women choose to identify more with their race than their gender. As bell hooks wrote in *Ain't I a Woman?*, the feminist movement "exposed the fact that white women were not willing to relinquish their support of white supremacy to support the interests of all women." During the 1972 presidential election, this friction materialized as indecision about supporting the only Black woman in the race, and more broadly within the feminist movement, which often failed to prioritize the needs of Black and brown women equally with those of white women.

In contrast to the conditional support from the white feminists, Chisholm's Black and Latino women supporters understood her request for an exclusive endorsement the first time she asked. These were women who knew how protracted and difficult a political fight could be, given their previous movement experiences. For Fannie Lou Hamer, her struggle included overcoming abuse and targeting in Mississippi. Lupe Anguiano went so far as to petition the Pope for an official separation from the church so that she could continue her advocacy and organizing work. And Gwendolyn Cherry felt every bump as she traversed the rocky road toward breaking barriers in Florida. Each of them understood.

Steinem finally picked a side just before the New York primary in April 1972. She felt the pressure to choose, referring to the decision as "fish-or-cut-bait," as both Chisholm and McGovern were running in the state. One phone call from McGovern was a death knell for Steinem's primary support for his campaign. During the call, McGovern expressed shock at how much money the women's movement raised during a recent fundraiser, and how much the feminist agenda appealed to voters. McGovern's surprise demonstrated his lack of understanding of the reach and power of the women's movement as a mobilizing force during the 1972 election cycle. After hearing McGovern's shock, Steinem decided to run as a New York delegate for Shirley Chisholm, the only Democratic primary candidate who understood the power of the women's movement and the importance of women existing in a world with equal rights, equal access, and equal opportunity. Steinem recalled in her memoir, *Outrageous Acts and Everyday Rebellions*, that McGovern's inability to fully understand that reality in the way that Chisholm did was what helped her decide to ultimately run as a Shirley Chisholm delegate. NOW Founder Betty Friedan joined Steinem as a delegate running to support Chisholm, and they put up a late, but visible, push to attract New Yorkers to vote for Chisholm's campaign. While they ultimately did not win delegate seats at the Democratic Convention, they did run on the ballot for Chisholm.

So, what was all the unnecessary posturing about if the white leaders of the feminist movement eventually ran as Chisholm delegates? According to Steinem's memoir, *Outrageous Acts and Everyday Rebellions*, it stemmed from concerns about Chisholm's viability as a presidential candidate, and their desire to influence the Democratic platform at the convention. For Steinem and Friedan, specifically, they were caught between Chisholm and the white male candidates whom they were tied to in the previous presidential election cycle in 1968, and whom they wanted to support again in 1972. They were also caught between the white women of the liberation movement who questioned whether or not Shirley Chisholm *should* be the first woman to seek the Democratic nomination. As Chisholm described it, "Half of them said she should run while the other half said she shouldn't. The latter half wanted to see a white woman run for the nomination first." She believed that racism was the determining factor. With that level of internal division, hedging satisfied the segment of white feminists who didn't want to see the movement go all in with a Black woman's presidential campaign, but who didn't want to *be seen* dissenting against the only woman in the race. The decision also enabled visible leaders such as Steinem and Friedan to develop a well-reported and documented track record of supporting one of the eventual front runners, so that they could have a substantive presence at the Democratic Convention, where they sought to have a hand in developing the party's official platform. As they say, choices were made.

Another "choice" that was central to Shirley Chisholm's campaign was the choice of identity—which part of her identity to prioritize, and when. During her presidential campaign announcement speech, Shirley Chisholm boldly declared, in part, "I am not the candidate of Black America, though I am Black and proud. I am not the candidate of the women's movement of this country, although I am a woman and I'm equally proud of that...I am the candidate of the people of America." Translation: Don't try to box me in based on what you see. Still, that choice of racial and gender identity came to a head within the inclusive coalition that was developing around Chisholm's California campaign.

On one side were the women of the liberation movement who were predominantly white, middle-class, and key fundraisers for the campaign. The feminist volunteers, who were an extension of the National Organization for Women, were quick to organize community meetings in support of the campaign even before Chisholm made her official announcement. They launched the required petitions and signature drives to get Chisholm on the ballot in states across the nation. And because of their central role in getting the campaign going in local communities, they believed that they deserved to have an outsized role in setting the campaign's priorities and direction—which was an uninformed and shortsighted thought. On the other side of this coalition equation were the Black people who were organizing for Chisholm across the nation, working to convince their elders and religious leaders that a Black person and a woman with vision was not a threat, but a leader. They were focused on issues of survival related to quality education, housing, health care, and food security. A number of Chisholm's Black volunteers, separately from the Black Panthers, initially collaborated with the white feminists on organizing and campaigning efforts in California, but tensions rose quickly as the Black volunteers refused to play second fiddle to the white women organizers. As Chisholm described it, "They fought like cats and dogs... The white women would say, 'We're putting her up for President, we're raising most of the money... we should say what's important and what's not important.' And the Black people would say, 'She's one of us. She's our sister.'" In spite of all of this strife, Chisholm refused to intervene.

What the NOW supporters failed to realize was that supporting a campaign didn't equate to control of said campaign. And it most certainly doesn't grant one demographic group of supporters dominion over another—especially when the groups involved have been historically marginalized, subjugated, and prohibited from living with the basic human rights afforded to white men.

The tensions between the white feminists and the Black organizers weren't unique to California. In Florida, during a tour of the state before Chisholm officially announced her candidacy, organizers arranged for a celebratory welcome motorcade of 100 cars with placards to meet Chisholm and her team at a local airport ahead of a youth rally. The motorcade participants walked to the tarmac and waited to greet Chisholm and her staff as they deplaned. As soon as they arrived, the crowd of white and Black supporters who had gathered rushed to greet Chisholm. Almost immediately, the white supporters surrounded Chisholm and started to usher her to their waiting cars at the front of the motorcade. In response, the Black supporters protested by shouting, "She is a sister," indicating that *they* wanted the honor of leading the motorcade and driving her to the event. Finger pointing and shouting fed the argument, and the commotion swelled around Chisholm as she stood waiting for someone to simply take her to the rally. Eventually, she spotted a man standing outside of the crowd wearing a "CHIZUM for President" hat, and she asked him to drive her to the rally while her other supporters were "fighting and fussing" behind her.

Chisholm wanted no part of the tussle, and she certainly wasn't going to decide which faction she would ride with in that heated moment, so she excused herself. Similar to the California infighting, Chisholm refused to intervene in Florida. She believed that every disagreement between her Black and white supporters was an extension of both identity groups attempting to claim her and control her. She also understood that the optics of seemingly siding with either of the groups would risk the support of the other group. Thus, she stayed back and hoped that the factions would sort it out themselves—effectively hedging on her own leadership responsibilities. In this airport scenario, the arguing supporters figured it out only after she'd left with that lone supporter who misspelled her name on his hat.

Back in California, tensions reached a fever pitch. The National Organization for Women volunteers and Black campaign volunteers clashed regularly. As Chisholm recalled, California was full of "bitter hostility" between the white women and the Black organizers. There were parade routes that cut out stops in Black communities without notice or discussion. There were allegedly physical threats made between volunteers. And there was a tenor of dismissiveness about the specific concerns of each demographic group as "the women didn't want me to discuss what the Black people were talking about. The Black people didn't want any of the women's programs." These ongoing tensions reflected the desperation and angst between the two groups that were effectively fighting for oxygen within the sole campaign that attempted to engage them all in a substantive way. One could easily chalk it up to decades of disenfranchisement and disregard from standing political figures. Now that both groups had a champion, a candidate who empowered them, they wanted exclusive rights to her space, her time, and her platform.

For the white feminists, that fight for oxygen and attention materialized in their push to have abortion rights featured as a clear plank in the official platform. Unfortunately for them, McGovern went back and forth on the issue throughout the primary campaign. He'd initially stated that abortion was a private matter, and that "laws should not stand in the way" of its implementation. Additionally, in a questionnaire McGovern completed for *Ms.* magazine, he expressed support for the "repeal of all state laws governing abortion." But as late as May 1972, two months before the Democratic National Convention, McGovern denied that he supported abortions, even bringing a Catholic priest and Kathleen Kennedy, the daughter of Robert Kennedy, on the campaign trail to appeal to conservative Midwestern voters. It was the type of desperate political flip-flopping that proved that McGovern was willing to acquiesce on politically charged, divisive issues in the name of winning votes—principles and promises be damned. It was also a disappointing blow to the feminists who supported McGovern's campaign. They had to have felt a degree of embarrassment after being lied to so blatantly and publicly. But for whatever reason, they didn't give up all hope.

Even after McGovern "waffled," as Gloria Steinem described it, she and leading feminists still believed that they could negotiate abortion-related language for inclusion in the Democratic platform. One month before the convention, Steinem, Friedan, and members of the National Women's Political Caucus met with McGovern and his aides to discuss options. Steinem even suggested the language "reproductive freedom" to replace "abortion." And while McGovern listened politely to their perspectives, he had already made his anti-abortion shift.

To make matters worse, during the convention, when it appeared that the "reproductive freedom" language in the policy platform was gaining momentum among delegates, McGovern's team actively lobbied against the language. The move breached yet another commitment with the feminist leaders as McGovern's team previously committed to allowing delegates to "vote their conscience" when it came to abortion. All trust was lost. The feminist leaders had given their political power to McGovern, and for what? A diluted policy plank for women that omitted the right to bodily autonomy and access to basic health care in the form of an abortion.

Considering that the Supreme Court decided *Roe v. Wade* and protected the constitutional right to access abortion in January 1973, one would think that abortion rights were ultimately protected. Think again. The 2016 election presented voters with an opportunity to elect a woman president of the United States as Democrats selected Hillary Clinton as their nominee. Similar to Shirley Chisholm, Clinton faced a barrage of sexism as a woman candidate, a trait that proved an insurmountable barrier even for some women voters. Interviews of white women voters revealed particularly negative sentiments around Clinton's candidacy, from women stating "I don't know if I trust her," to "It's almost insulting that people think we're going to choose a candidate because she's the same sex as us." And then there was the concern that Clinton seemed too smart, as one voter said, "...it seems a very intellectual thing, but it doesn't feel to me as if it is coming from her heart." With these sentiments front and center, 47 percent of white women voted for Donald Trump in the 2016 general election. At no point was it assumed that Clinton would have the support of all white women in the nation, but this plurality of support occurred in spite of the recording of Trump describing grabbing women by their genitals, the numerous alleged sexual assault victims who stepped forward during his campaign (and since, as Trump was found liable of sexually abusing E. Jean Carroll in 2023), and his endorsements from the Ku Klux Klan and white supremacists. The 47 percent of white women, along with the 62 percent of white men, who voted for Trump believed an apparent white supremacist and accused sexual predator should hold the highest office in the country.

As a result, a former reality TV show host was elected and proceeded to stack the Supreme Court with three conservative, anti-abortion justices in an effort to overturn *Roe v. Wade*. Unfortunately, he achieved that goal in the summer of 2022 when the Supreme Court overturned the constitutional right to access abortion, nullifying fifty years of precedent, to the detriment of women and people with uteruses across the nation. Trump was so proud of his work that in 2024, during his third presidential campaign, he emphasized that he alone orchestrated the overturn of *Roe v. Wade*. All the while, attacks on reproductive freedoms spread beyond abortions, including the criminalization of miscarriages and in-vitro fertilization. As a result of Trump and his supporters' efforts, twenty-one states in the nation have implemented either complete bans on abortions or bans as early as six weeks, often well before a pregnant person even knows that they are pregnant. Physicians and hospital administrators report being so confused about, and fearful of violating, the abortion bans that they are refusing basic health care to women who require critical care. There are reports of women experiencing miscarriages in hospital lobbies and giving birth to underdeveloped fetuses in their cars after being turned away from medical establishments. Survivors of sexual assault are being forced to carry unwanted pregnancies to term due to lack of access to abortion care. And there are women whose lives are at risk because the bans prevent physicians from providing abortion care after their pregnancies have been deemed unviable.

One lesson that can be gleaned from both the 1972 and the 2016 elections is that hedging one's support, especially when occupying a position of cultural influence, does not reduce political risks; it leads to losses for everyone. Losses in substantive commitments, losses in political power, and losses in our most basic rights and freedoms. Shirley Chisholm knew that, and it was why she requested full, committed support from the people who backed her. She demanded solidarity while she shook the political system wide awake.

To avoid these losses in the future, coalitions must be formed with stakeholders who are fully aligned behind a singular mission, across race, gender identity, and age. Such unity is what reinforces coalitions against the blowback that comes with challenging traditional power structures. In 1972, the white feminists of the moment weren't able to provide that degree of fortitude. Their capacity was limited to a respectful appearance at a party, or divided support between Chisholm and a white male elected official who was uncommitted to the cause. And because Chisholm understood the impact of their limitations, she was clear in communicating her ultimatum when she declared, "...If you can't support me, or you can't endorse me, then get out of my way. You do your thing, and let me do mine."

CHAPTER EIGHT

THE SISTERHOOD

"She is a friend of mine. She gather me, man. The pieces I am, she gather them and give them back to me in all the right order."

—Toni Morrison, *Beloved*

When Barbara Lee arrived late to the Welcome to Hollywood party with Huey P. Newton, she couldn't have imagined experiencing a more significant introduction that night than the one she was responsible for facilitating between Congresswoman Chisholm and Huey P. Newton. Little did Lee know, she was about to meet the woman who would later become her self-described "sister in the struggle." Given the late hour, the party's guests had migrated to the veranda and the pool area in Diahann Carroll's backyard oasis, and while they mingled, one local community activist and fundraising organizer was left to answer the front door as the last few attendees arrived. That activist was none other than Maxine Waters.

Today we know Maxine Waters as the long-serving congresswoman representing Southern Los Angeles County, California, who suffers no fools and does not mince words. Many may recall Representative Waters famously shutting down the ill-prepared Treasury Secretary Steve Mnuchin during a Congressional Financial Services Committee hearing in 2017. Seemingly unwilling to cooperate and coherently respond to Representative Waters' line of questioning, Mnuchin repeatedly attempted to run out the hearing clock by offering long-winded, meandering responses. Waters, undeterred, refused to allow him to dictate the pace of the hearing. Each time Mnuchin began rambling, Waters immediately declared clearly and firmly, "Reclaiming my time," much to Mnuchin's exasperation. The phrase quickly went viral online and entered the meme-able lexicon of Black women across the country. For many, this was their introduction to Congresswoman Waters, who has held her seat in Congress since 1990.

Waters applied that same tone of engagement to the man who targeted her in 2018 after she called for peaceful protests against his administration—one Donald Trump. The call was in response to the inhumane policy of separating families that were seeking asylum at the US-Mexico border. Part of Donald Trump's targeting included social media posts in which he wrote that Waters "called for harm" against his supporters. He even issued a threat: "Be careful what you wish for, Max." As a result of his online posts, Waters received several death threats in the days that followed, and she was forced to cancel multiple campaign events due to safety concerns. When Waters did return to the event stage for a pro-immigration rally in Los Angeles, California, she was resolute, "If you shoot me, you better shoot straight. There's nothing like a wounded animal." Her statement was a heartbreaking reflection of the violence and targeted hate lobbed against her for daring to stand up to a president who did his best to defile and desecrate the office he held. Moreover, it was a reflection of her fortitude and power.

Maxine Waters' trademark resolve was steeped in her experiences as an advocate and fundraiser in the Watts community of Los Angeles, California, during the late 1960s and early 1970s. Watts was still recovering from the rebellion of August 1965, which started after police pulled over Marquette Frye two blocks from his home on suspicion of drunk driving. Afraid, Frye's brother ran home and awoke their mother to come to his aid. When Mrs. Frye attempted to intervene in the police forcibly arresting Marquette, the officers struck her in the head with a nightstick before arresting her, too. A crowd started to gather as the scene unfolded, and the witnesses were incensed by the police violence, which they saw as an extension of the long-standing tension between police and the largely Black, low-income community. What followed was six days of rioting, which prompted California leaders to deploy 14,000 national guardsmen to Watts. The riots resulted in nearly 3,500 arrests, 34 deaths, and millions of dollars in property damage.

While the press and local leaders attempted to pin the spark of the riots exclusively on the traffic stop and Marquette Frye's arrest, this rebellion signified the broader desperation of the Black residents of Watts. It was a direct response to police brutality as well as the harsh conditions that Black residents were experiencing as they were forced to live without quality jobs, stable resources, or the investment and attention that they needed from state leaders. An official commission launched by then-California Governor Pat Brown to investigate the causes of the uprising confirmed that the events in Watts were an "explosion" in response to communal distress, and that "it is part of an American problem." The commission's recommendations included the creation of job training programs in partnership with the local and state government, investments in preschool education programs and reducing class sizes at schools, and the development of nonconfrontational connections between the local community and the police department. Unfortunately, these recommendations were not implemented in the years after the uprising.

In 1965, Waters worked as a teacher and community facilitator for the Watts Head Start program, which offered free educational services for children from birth to five years old. She was also a leader for the Mothers of Watts, a community group that emerged after the 1965 Watts Rebellion and offered financial and housing support to single mothers. Through her work, she cultivated deep relationships within the Black community in and around Los Angeles, and her reputation as an effective community leader grew to the point that she began volunteering, campaigning, and fundraising for political candidates. By the early 1970s, Waters had worked on the campaigns of California leaders including Tom Bradley, the first Black mayor of Los Angeles, and had served as campaign manager of David Cunningham Jr.'s successful run for the Los Angeles City Council.

Considering that the Welcome to Hollywood party was Shirley Chisholm's sole high-dollar Los Angeles fundraiser, it is only fitting that Waters, a well-connected community activist and skilled political fundraiser, had a hand in coordinating the lavish event. Waters was trusted to greet guests at Diahann Carroll's doorstep, and by the time she first met Barbara Lee, Waters' work in politics and advocacy preceded her. Lee knew of Waters' efforts to gain additional resources for struggling single mothers; however, since Lee had never seen Waters before, she didn't recognize her at the moment the door opened. All of her attention was on introducing Huey P. Newton to Shirley Chisholm.

After a quick exchange of hellos, Waters escorted Newton and Lee directly into the throng of supporters surrounding the black tile pool. Lee knew that she liked Waters immediately, noting that Waters moved with a "sense of command over what she was doing." Plus, she was thrilled to see and interact with another Black woman in a visible role in California politics in 1972, and she was intentional about preserving the memory of meeting Waters. Waters was someone who could (and eventually did) serve as a mentor and a guide to Lee as she was developing her own political voice, especially as she learned to confidently wield political power while navigating the tensions between Chisholm's Black campaign volunteers and her white feminist supporters.

It was a gift for twenty-five-year-old Lee to know and interact with Black women leaders like Chisholm and Waters who could guide her through the convoluted shifts of politics and life. Chisholm herself had not been afforded the luxury of having predecessors who understood her experience while she charted the lonely path of making history as a Black woman in politics. And she most certainly did not have access to a sustained support system or safe space when she first arrived in Congress. Yes, she had her husband, Conrad Chisholm, in whom she could confide, and yes, she had supporters on the campaign trail who cheered her on. Still, she did not have an active, consistent network of support to comfort and to shield her from the indecencies and trials that came along with being the first to occupy institutions that were not built with Black people or women in mind. She did not have anyone more tenured to show her the way. What Chisholm needed was sisterhood.

Sisterhood is both a balm and a source of power. It is the protective covering that aids in one's healing, providing even the slightest respite amid trauma. It's the reassurance that someone will be there to support you when you take a risk. It's also the verbal backup in a room full of men who are attempting to interrupt you. And it's the visible loyalty and partnership that can drive political action.

Chisholm especially needed sisterhood during her first months on Capitol Hill, when she was verbally harassed and bullied in the Capitol Building by some of her colleagues who attempted to put her in her place. She described her early days in the House of Representatives as "miserable." On the House floor, one member repeatedly challenged her salary—the same salary the white men in Congress earned—each time she passed his desk. He would shout at her, with a thick Southern drawl, "Forty-two five," referring to the annual salary for members of Congress. Eventually, Chisholm told him that if he was so bothered by her presence and her equal salary, then he should "disappear when he sees her coming."

The disrespect Chisholm experienced on the House floor only escalated. One member who sat in an aisle seat would cough furiously as she approached her seat. Every day, he would watch her come onto the House floor, and start his hacking routine. Confused, and concerned for the man's health, Chisholm approached Representative Brock Adams from Washington State and inquired why someone hadn't helped this congressman who appeared to be suffering from a condition like tuberculosis. Adams explained to Chisholm that it was she who had to take action, revealing that this member was not only timing his cough to Chisholm's movements, but also pretending to spit on Chisholm by spitting into his handkerchief each time she passed him on the way to her seat on the House floor. While Adams was willing to demonstrate some degree of civility by informing Chisholm of the full picture of this disgusting greeting, his failure to intervene on her behalf is another reminder of the lack of sustained support that Chisholm experienced as the first Black woman to serve in Congress.

Chisholm, being the fighter that she was, came prepared the next day, armed with a handkerchief stuffed in the pocket of her sweater suit. As she entered the floor and the member began to cough, Chisholm mimicked his actions. Just as he was about to spit into his handkerchief toward Chisholm's face, she spat into her handkerchief and told him, "Beat you to it today." Reporters erupted in laughter from the press gallery, signaling that they, like Adams, were well aware of the offending congressman's pattern of behavior and that they agreed that he deserved his comeuppance. And yet the press cycle lacked any coverage about the daily abuses Chisholm faced on the Hill, where relationship building was essential to having substantive, legislative success.

Beyond the House floor, social spaces were repeatedly made hostile by Chisholm's colleagues. In the congressional cafeteria, there was an unspoken rule that seating was assigned by state delegation. Even so, Chisholm routinely ate her lunch alone with a newspaper at any table she could find, unknowingly violating the lunchroom rule. Merely exercising autonomy in where she wanted to sit garnered harassment by a member from Georgia, who one day tried to force her to move. Too hungry and unwilling to budge, Chisholm advised the Georgia representative to sit at a different table, and told him, "If anybody bothers you, you tell them to see Shirley Chisholm." Oddly, the congressman obliged and skulked off to a different table.

In each of these scenarios, Chisholm was forced to respond alone, without any backup. And while she was not the first woman of color elected to the House of Representatives, her reception was representative of how the predominantly white male–led chamber viewed Black women as prime targets for harassment and abuse. In stark contrast, the first woman of color, and the first Asian American woman, elected to Congress, Representative Patsy Takemoto Mink of Hawaii, received a much more welcoming introduction to Washington than Shirley Chisholm.

Prior to her election to Congress, Mink, a Japanese American attorney, experienced racism and discrimination throughout her life. As a student at the University of Nebraska, she campaigned to desegregate the dormitories after she was forced to live in the "International House," with other students of color, despite being a US citizen. Within one year, the campus dorms were desegregated. And after being rejected from a dozen medical schools, she was forced to pivot to studying law. When she arrived at the University of Chicago Law School, she was classified as an international student though she was a US citizen. The discrimination continued after Mink earned her law degree in 1951, as she was repeatedly denied work because she was a married woman and a mother. In response, she established her own law firm.

After more than a decade of organizing Democrats within the Young Democrats of America and the local territorial government of Hawaii, Mink won election to Congress in 1964, where Washington welcomed her with open arms. Immediately, the press dubbed Mink "Congress' New Glamour Girl," and described her as "delicate and dainty." The political elite also embraced her, including President Lyndon Johnson and Vice President Hubert Humphrey. The same members of Congress who welcomed Mink went on to target Chisholm. While Mink advocated for education programs, for funding for childcare programs, for gender equity, and against air strikes in Vietnam—stances identical to Shirley Chisholm's—Mink was met with a courteous reception from her congressional colleagues while Chisholm was seen as an unwelcome rebel. Mink went so far as to describe the men in Congress as being "just as gallant as the men in Hawaii—and that goes double for Lyndon Johnson." The difference in reception between Mink and Chisholm can be attributed to the inappropriate objectification of Mink, which was reflected in the headlines and descriptions, as well as white supremacist efforts to distinguish and embrace Asian Americans as part of the model minority myth while continuing to denigrate Black people. The model minority concept—that in spite of experiencing horrific discrimination and targeted crimes, Japanese Americans still found success—had been introduced into society in 1966 by William Petersen. Whether consciously, or unconsciously, the white men in Washington, DC, had fully bought in to the notion, given their disparate treatment of Mink and Chisholm. Mink was sexualized and infantilized, while Chisholm was villainized and disregarded. Still, the two women found ways to collaborate with each other.

When Chisholm joined Mink in Congress in 1969, the two collaborated on legislation related to gender equity, tax fairness, and civil rights, including Title IX, which prohibits gender-based exclusion and discrimination in all aspects of education programs at institutions that receive federal support. Title IX lives on today as the college sports equalizer, but its expansive provisions also apply to admissions, scholarships, employment, and safety protections. Mink was denied many of these protections when she was rejected from twelve medical schools because she was a woman.

In addition to their legislative collaborations, Mink also joined Chisholm as a candidate in the 1972 Democratic primary election, vying for the party nomination for president of the United States. While their campaign intentions differed—Chisholm was focused on coalition building and garnering enough delegates to influence the Democratic Party platform, and Mink was intent on declaring her anti-war position by participating in a single primary competition—they coordinated their efforts so that they did not directly compete against each other. Unlike the white feminists, there was no false or augmented support between Mink and Chisholm, only respectful competition. Hawaii did not have delegates to send to the Democratic Convention, so Mink ran an active campaign in Oregon. As Mink crisscrossed Oregon, Chisholm made as many stops as she could in the fourteen states where she was on the ballot.

While Mink and Chisholm did collaborate, their dynamic was not one of total support, as Chisholm was left to respond to the affronts from her colleagues alone. Given the personal dynamics at play, it would be plausible that Mink was less apt to risk her social capital for Chisholm. It is an enticing proposition to imagine an alternate scenario where Chisholm had Black, Asian, and Latina congresswomen to stand beside her in each moment of harassment. Women who could affirm that she was not imagining the abuse, nor overreacting to it. Women who could stand up to the bullies. Imagine for a moment that the same Black and Latina feminists who fully supported Chisholm during her presidential run were with Chisholm as she entered Congress in January 1969. Fannie Lou Hamer, Lupe Anguiano, and

Gwendolyn Cherry would have been the perfect revolutionary leaders to back Shirley Chisholm in real time. Hamer knew how to raise her voice in protest and illustrate the visceral, human impact of inaction. Anguiano was adept at mobilizing support and coalition building across issues and race. And Cherry understood exactly how to stand firmly, and fully, in her power as an equal citizen, and how to empower others to do the same.

They would have all been able to carry some portion of the burden that Chisholm faced day in and day out by directly intervening on her behalf during, or before, each inhumane incident. And after each confrontation, this same group would have also been there to decompress with Chisholm, releasing the pressure valve that comes with merely existing and functioning as a Black woman in historically white male dominated spaces. Knowing Shirley Chisholm, they could have even found humor in the absurd behaviors of these grown men who managed to be elected as representatives. Moreover, they would have been able to accelerate the political reset that Chisholm was driving as an activist leader.

The nation has seen these types of interactions, and sisterhood interventions, up close in recent years. Consider the moment in 2024 when Representative Alexandria Ocasio-Cortez of New York intervened on behalf of Representative Jasmine Crockett of Texas after Representative Marjorie Taylor Greene of Georgia made an inappropriate comment about Crockett's appearance. Without hesitation, Ocasio-Cortez came to Crockett's defense, introducing a motion to strike Greene's words from the Congressional Record, and demanding she apologize to Crockett, in accordance with the rules of the House of Representatives. This real-time backup provided cover for Crockett, and when Greene attempted to further escalate the matter, Crockett shot back with a hypothetical question about a "bleach blonde, bad-built butch body," creating a viral internet moment analogous to Chisholm's handkerchief move. While Crockett's question was well received, it must also be stated that the derogatory use of the word "butch" is harmful to the lesbian community, who don't deserve to be the butt of a joke. Still, this is the type of support that Congresswoman Chisholm needed as her colleagues pretended to spit in her face and questioned her equal salary. Unfortunately, in 1969, she faced this uphill battle alone.

Thankfully, the uncomfortable solitude of being the only Black woman in the House chamber did not deter Chisholm from bucking the system on her own. She began her term by challenging House leadership and petitioning to have her committee assignment changed. Originally, she was assigned to the House Agriculture Committee and Forestry Subcommittee, which she believed was ridiculous as she represented Brooklyn, New York. She had no interest in developing legislation related to forests when Brooklyn had more concrete than trees. Chisholm was adamant about serving on a committee that reflected her previous experiences and expertise as an educator and reflected the needs of the community that she represented. After protesting on the House floor, where the chair refused to recognize her for several minutes, her request to be reassigned was accepted, and she was ultimately appointed to the Veteran Affairs Committee. She also regularly outdebated her congressional colleagues on issues from job training programs to the war in Vietnam. With her consistent, visible action, Chisholm interrupted the tone and day-to-day operations of the House of Representatives. She spoke up for what she believed in from the moment she entered the chamber, something her colleagues described as "political suicide." While their comments were meant to dismiss her, they foreshadowed that Chisholm was making waves in a manner that others weren't willing to, and her steadfast approach became an even bigger part of her public appeal.

Chisholm's unflinching posture also effectively softened the ground for the Black and brown women congressional leaders who followed her. Their declarations and explicit statements of dissent were more readily accepted, and probably more expected, as a result of Chisholm's leadership. Barbara Jordan, the first Southern Black woman to be elected to Congress in 1972, and the first Black woman elected to the Texas State House, stood up as a defender of the Constitution, and as a proponent of justice and accountability during the impeachment proceedings of President Richard Nixon in July 1974. Her eleven-minute televised opening statement was well received, especially as Nixon had become increasingly unpopular as the layers of the Watergate scandal were peeled back during congressional investigations and hearings.

She directly admonished Nixon's intentional, conscious efforts to undermine the Constitution, and she aptly framed the importance of the impeachment proceedings. Jordan was an intellectual and political force in her own right, and because she walked along the path that Chisholm had carved as an unabashed truth teller, members of Congress and the public were primed to receive another Black woman as she delivered a scathing and honest speech about the president. With her statement, Jordan explicitly called out that the Constitution's opening phrase—"We the People"—did not originally include her, or any woman or Black person. But in this scenario, Jordan, a Black woman, would be heard clearly on the matter.

Moreover, Jordan had support from other Black women in Congress at the time. In 1974, that included Representative Yvonne Braithwaite Burke, the first Black woman from California elected to Congress in 1972 and the first member of Congress to give birth and take maternity leave. There was also Representative Cardiss Collins, the first Black woman from Illinois elected to Congress in 1973, following the unexpected death of her husband, Representative George Collins. This was the first era in Congress where multiple Black women could see and lean on each other while doing their political work. While the first four Black women in Congress were each individuals who "did not move in lock step," they were able to share advice and their frustrations with each other. Congresswoman Burke shared with the *Chicago Tribune* that Shirley Chisholm was "'incredibly good' in spelling out some of the pitfalls [of Congress]," especially related to the media coverage. It was invaluable advice that Chisholm would have appreciated herself as a freshman member. Congresswomen Jordan and Chisholm were equally committed to upending the rules of Congress, rules that they both disdained. Jordan specifically believed that the rules "deprive[d] individual members of power and concentrate[d] it in committees." As Chisholm had her previous run-in with committee assignments, she understood Jordan's sentiment, and they could back each other up in the endeavor to change the rules.

As the new Black congresswomen widened the pathway that had been established for them by Shirley Chisholm, their mutual support became a new layer of reassurance and comfort for Black women within the storied halls of Congress. The increase in numbers also strengthened how the women were each perceived individually and how they each defined their time in Congress as they moved beyond being tokenized to being respected as leaders. There was a noticeable shift in the press coverage that emphasized their skills. Jordan was described as a "masterful politician," and Burke was celebrated for breaking barriers. Unfortunately, that praise often came in contrast to Shirley Chisholm's coverage, which was almost always served with a side of criticism, including describing Chisholm as "screeching and emotional." It appeared that once members of the media decided their perspectives about Chisholm, they refused to shift. Instead, they doubled down in an effort to paint her as a negative alternative to the Black women who were elected after her.

By 1998, there were 56 women serving in the House of Representatives, including 13 Black women, 1 Asian woman, and 4 Latinas. One of those women included Chisholm's mentee and former campaign staffer, Barbara Lee, who was elected to Congress during the 1998 special election to replace Representative Ron Dellums, a longtime Chisholm supporter. While women winning more House seats signaled progress since Chisholm's fraught and isolated early days as a congresswoman, this limited number of seats represented only 13 percent of the House at a time when women comprised a majority of the US population. So it was still a far cry from "equal representation" for women in Congress.

One of the Black women in that group of 56 congresswomen was Maxine Waters. Waters and Barbara Lee's political careers had run in staggered parallel through the years following the Welcome to Hollywood party. Waters first ascended to the California State Assembly in Sacramento in 1976 and then to Congress in 1990. On a similar trajectory, Lee was elected to the California Assembly in 1990, the California State Senate in 1996, and Congress in 1998. With each progression in her political career, Lee enjoyed endorsements and advice from Shirley Chisholm and Maxine Waters. Even as Lee was sworn in as a state senator, Chisholm was on hand to tease her protégée in a speech. Lee beamed as Chisholm walked to the podium to shower her with praise on her election to the California State Assembly. Ever the jokester, Chisholm recounted how in 1972 she admonished Lee for not being registered to vote and called her a "little girl." Chisholm also joked about how, years later, Lee followed her around and hung on her every word before working up the courage to ask Chisholm if she could run her presidential campaign operations in Northern California. Coming from anyone else, this nickname and recollection would be seen as derogatory and infantilizing. But between two Black women with a long-shared history, Chisholm was reminding Lee, in two simple words, of how far the young freedom fighter had truly come.

During Lee's campaign in the 1998 special election race to fill retiring Congressman Ron Dellums' seat in the House of Representatives, Waters was on the ground in Oakland, California, campaigning for Lee and mobilizing voters. She also championed Lee in the press, describing her as a "rising star" as she entered Congress. This was invaluable support from a Black woman who understood the political struggle and was excited to lift up another Black woman ascending in her own career. For Lee, Waters lending her voice translated into fewer barriers to traverse during the campaign, and confidence that she would have sustained support and partnership to confront hardships that arose during her term.

As Barbara Lee got settled on Capitol Hill, she and Maxine Waters worked in tandem on some of the biggest moments in Congress at the turn of the millennium. First, there was a coordinated intervention in the Elián González international custody case in late 1999 and early 2000. Elián González was a six-year-old boy who was discovered and rescued from an inflatable tube off the coast of Florida in November 1999. Elián had been traveling with his mother, who tragically died during a storm, and twelve other refugees as they attempted to immigrate to the United States by crossing the ninety miles of ocean between Cuba and Florida via a small boat. After Elián was treated at a hospital in Florida, the Immigration and Naturalization

Service released him to extended family members in Miami, instead of returning him to his father, Juan Miguel González, in Cuba. This triggered an international custody battle about which family members had rights to care for Elián as his parents were no longer together at the time of his mother's death, and which national government had the right to determine custody. It was a highly visible crisis that dominated the global press for months. The custody and diplomatic questions involved in this case brought on contentious debates, and the nation stood divided.

As part of the efforts to intervene in this decision, Lee and Waters traveled to Cuba to meet with Elián's father in January 2000. In the same week, they escorted Elián's grandmothers through Capitol Hill to meet with other members of Congress. Their engagement was a marker of their political prominence as well as their ability to substantively engage with the human traumas associated with this sensitive, emotional battle. While the media used Elián and the custody debate as a political football, Waters and Lee took the time to sit down with Elián's father and his grandmothers to understand their perspectives and their desire to have their child and grandson returned home to his father's care. By standing together, Waters and Lee had each other as reinforcement as they took a stance on the issue that many Americans were beginning to reach—that Elián should be with his father, his remaining biological parent. After intervention from then–Attorney General Janet Reno, federal agents with the Immigration and Naturalization Service conducted a traumatic raid with guns drawn, took Elián from his extended family, and returned him to his father's custody.

Later that year, Maxine Waters and Barbara Lee found themselves working together on the congressional certification of the 2000 presidential election, five weeks after Election Day. The 2000 presidential election between Vice President Al Gore and then-Governor George W. Bush was controversial from start to finish. But it grew particularly fraught on Election Night as television networks wrongly called the Florida outcome in Bush's favor, then reversed their on-air determinations. The Florida votes showed Bush winning the state by 0.03 percent, or 1,784 votes out of 5.95 million votes. Given the tight margin, a machine recount was automatically triggered, and the recount began the day after the election. Simultaneously, both campaigns hired attorneys in preparation for a legal battle that would ultimately, and unfortunately, decide the election.

While Gore's campaign filed a lawsuit to allow time for a hand recount in four Florida counties, Bush's campaign filed suit to stop the recount altogether. In the midst of the legal fight, which advanced to the US Supreme Court, Republican organizers manufactured a violent protest among predominantly white male supporters that targeted the Miami-Dade County Election Offices and officials. On November 22, 2000, violent rioters chased election officials, punched and trampled volunteers, and attempted to break down the doors to the election supervisor's office. As the violent riot was unfolding, Miami-Dade election officials voted unanimously to end the recount—a precursor of sorts to the Republicans who protested and demanded that election workers "stop the count" in battleground states during the 2020 presidential election, and the violent insurrection in the US Capitol on January 6, 2021. Weeks later, the US Supreme Court ruled 5–4 that there could be no further count of disputed ballots in Florida, effectively calling the election for George W. Bush. Al Gore promptly conceded the election. In his concession speech, Gore communicated his frustration with the court, and his commitment to certifying the election noting, "Let there be no doubt, while I strongly disagree with this court's decision, I accept it. I accept the finality of this outcome which will be ratified... in the electoral college." By peacefully expressing both his dissent and respect for the court's decision, Gore offered a stark contrast to the violence from Republicans who targeted Florida election officials, and, later, Donald Trump's reaction to losing the 2020 presidential election.

Because members of the House of Representatives are responsible for certifying the electoral college votes, Maxine Waters and Barbara Lee and members of the House of Representatives leveraged the vote count process as an opportunity to register their peaceful dissent to the Supreme Court's ruling as the ballots for Florida were presented on the House floor. Representative Maxine Waters rose to state her objection to "the fraudulent twenty-five Florida electoral college votes." When Gore asked if the objection was in writing and signed by a member of the House and a US senator, which is procedurally required to officially register an objection to the electoral college vote, Waters replied, "The objection is in writing, and I don't care that it is not signed by a member of the Senate." With a witty tone, Gore responded that "... the rules do care." Waters was prepared to reject congressional rules in the name of the voters, and she was immediately followed by Representative Barbara Lee, who declared that "... it was the Supreme Court and not the people of the United States who decided this election."

In a powerful demonstration of solidarity, eighteen members of the House, almost exclusively Black and Asian representatives, joined Waters and Lee in registering their objections. One by one, they emphasized the "misconduct," the "violation of the Voting Rights Act," and the "disenfranchisement of millions of voters." None of their objections could officially be registered, as no single senator would sign them. But by going on the record, publicly, they were making it clear to the American people that they were fighting for the people's rights in real time. Maxine Waters returned to the floor on two additional occasions to request a withdrawal from the joint session, and to requisition an extension of the debate, both futile but the final portion of the protest effort. As the objections to the Florida electoral college votes concluded, Florida Representative Alcee Hastings shouted to Gore from the House floor, "We did all we could," and with a chuckle, Gore expressed his thanks.

This coordinated effort, spearheaded by Black women, demonstrated the impact of collective action in the name of the people for all the nation to see. There was no way a lone dissenter could have executed this peaceful protest, but through planning among women and their peers, Congress stood up in the name of democracy. And while the protests concluded and George W. Bush officially became the president, the display of sisterhood is what should linger in the mind of citizens who witnessed this moment.

In 2001, Representative Lee led the charge on a historic anti-war vote with global implications. Two days after the September 11, 2001, terrorist attack on the World Trade Center and the Pentagon, the deadliest attack on US soil, the official posture from the Bush administration to the world was, "We are at war." In a haze of fear and retaliation, Congress offered him nearly unanimous support to use "all necessary and appropriate force" to respond to the attack. Translation: Congress granted President Bush blanket permission to use the military and national resources however and whenever he determined it was necessary in order to "get" the people responsible for September 11th. Unfortunately, only one member of Congress had the courage to object to this at that moment. Congresswoman Barbara Lee cast the sole vote against the blanket authorization. Lee had witnessed the impact of the Vietnam War as a young person, a war without an expiration date, funded with a bottomless defense budget that siphoned resources from domestic priorities and needs. And she, similar to Shirley Chisholm, understood how a "blank check" for a president and the US military would harm the individuals sent to fight in aimless wars. As Lee wrote in her memoir, *Renegade for Peace and Justice*, "I knew then that the administration would turn it into a global war and tried to warn the nation and my colleagues in the Congress." Unfortunately, it took months before other members of Congress began to pause and question the lack of focus, the lack of evidence, and the lack of logic coming from the Bush administration. Meanwhile, the administration prepared to use the expansive military authorization it had been granted to initiate preemptive strikes in Iraq in March 2003.

As their worst fears were being realized, more members joined Barbara Lee in speaking up against the Bush administration. On the eve of the strikes, Representative Maxine Waters offered a statement on the House floor in which she forcefully questioned President Bush and his actions in Iraq. "Our own intelligence community headed by the CIA said that they could not find in Iraq that which was being described by our own Secretary of State," Waters stated. "Something is wrong with this picture." Within her criticism, Waters was careful to emphasize that she still supported the efforts to capture the terrorists behind September 11th, while admonishing the White House for not acting toward that explicit goal. In this delicate move, she was able to give a nod to Representative Lee's valid concerns about an unending war and urge the administration not to move forward with the strikes without evidence—which it failed to do.

After witnessing four years of the Bush administration's aimless efforts in Iraq, Representatives Barbara Lee and Maxine Waters joined with Representative Lynn Woolsey to co-found the "Out of Iraq" Caucus in 2005, which sought to publicly pressure the Bush White House to set a troop withdrawal timeline. In refusing to fund military operations in Iraq, this group of California congresswomen, dubbed "The Triad," effectively picked up the baton from Chisholm. They stood together, and they stood firm for years as some of the earliest voices to speak out against the Iraq War, and against the vast authorizations granted to Bush following September 11th. And while troops were not fully withdrawn from Iraq until 2011, the collaborative support system that "The Triad" fostered, and that Maxine Waters and Barbara Lee nurtured, was invaluable in this fight. These women banded together at a time when President Bush was unwilling to admit the failures of his preemptive attack, in order to plant the seed of reversing course and removing US troops and resources from Iraq.

Representatives Waters and Lee were the embodiment of what it could have looked like had Chisholm enjoyed sisterhood in Congress. They had each other to confer with as they advocated for Elián González, his father, and his grandmothers. They could strategize together in the cloak room before taking to the House floor to vocalize their objections about the 2000 presidential election. They coordinated their advocacy efforts to combat rogue missions by the Bush administration. They could roll their eyes at each other in response to the ridiculous statements from Republicans. At the most granular level, they had a sisterhood. And the most authentic part of their bond is rooted in the way that they demonstrated their trust in each other, and how they visibly supported each other on a range of issues—a trademark of a healthy sisterhood.

There is no way that Barbara Lee and Maxine Waters could have imagined their eventual sisterhood blossoming as much as it has since they met at Diahann Carroll's home in April 1972. To go from greeting one another at the door, to teaming up on resolving national and international issues, coordinating acts of civil disobedience, and sharing the burden of legislating and campaigning as Black women twenty-six years later is nothing short of remarkable. The journey they've taken together mirrors that of many long-term friendships between women, particularly between Black and brown women, where they've walked through fire and come out the other side better, stronger, and more united. This deeper level of connection derived from mutual respect and shared understanding is an integral ingredient for growing power, building communities, and serving the people with fortitude and clarity.

By joining forces, they extended the tradition of congressional sisterhood set by Barbara Jordan, Yvonne Braithwaite Burke, and Cardiss Collins when they joined Shirley Chisholm in Congress in 1972. And they helped set a blueprint via "The Triad," for the coordinated actions we see from today's leaders, such as Representatives Ayanna Pressley, Alexandria Ocasio-Cortez, Rashida Tlaib, and Ilhan Omar, also known as "The Squad." This sisterhood model among Black and brown women in Congress has spanned more than fifty years, and it has been a priceless asset for the members, and for the people as we build collective power.

CHAPTER NINE

THE LEGACY

"I've broken the ice."

—Shirley Chisholm, *Meet the Press*

On the eve of the 1972 Democratic National Convention in Miami, Florida, Shirley Chisholm walked onto the specially constructed set of NBC's *Meet the Press* wearing a blue-and-white knit sweater, a thick gold necklace, and an unshakable confidence in the presidential campaign that she had run for the previous seven months. She took her seat on the lower level of the two-tiered platform alongside four other Democratic primary election candidates, Senator George McGovern of South Dakota, Senator Hubert Humphrey of Minnesota, Senator Edmund Muskie of Maine, and Senator Henry Jackson of Washington. She was finally in her rightful position, among her peers, for the television broadcast—a position that she had to fight for in the courts after being denied by major news networks as well as the Federal Communications Commission. This two-hour, pre-convention NBC special would be Chisholm's first, and only, in-person, in-studio appearance with the other candidates. All the primary elections were finished before July 9, 1972, so this televised interaction was not a competitive debate, nor was it an appearance that would impact voters' decisions. Still, it was a significant on-air moment where Chisholm's presence would convey the impact of her campaign for the presidency and her contribution to disrupting the antiquated traditions of presidential politics.

During the interview, journalist Frank McGee asked, "Mrs. Chisholm, how do you account for the fact that no more Blacks than half have come to your cause in this primary process and now at the convention?" This journalist was operating under the assumption that being a Black candidate meant that Black voters would flock to Chisholm without a second thought. But his question was a reductive one that revealed his lack of understanding of Chisholm's history-defying presidential campaign. For context, Black people in the United States had gained increased access to the polls only seven years prior with the Voting Rights Act of 1965, and young people ages eighteen to twenty had gained the right to vote only months before the primary elections began in 1972. Not to mention the nearly two-centuries-old truth that only white men had ever run substantive campaigns for the presidency before the 1972 primary election. To gain half the votes of people who were voting for the very first time in their lives was nothing to scoff at, especially on live television.

Ever the teacher, Shirley Chisholm was happy to educate McGee. Sitting up as tall as her petite frame would allow, she tilted her head as she explained that no one in this nation had ever seen what she had done before. Her tone was matter-of-fact and crisp as she added, "It's a question of inculcation, reorientation, and education... you don't expect people—Black, white, men, or women—to suddenly overcome a tradition that has been steeped ever since the inception of this republic. So, I understand that. I've broken the ice."

Translation: Shirley Chisholm knew that she never had a chance of winning the Democratic nomination for president in 1972.

Chisholm lacked nearly every major ingredient required for a successful presidential campaign. She did not have money. She was outspent, by multiples, by the white men in the race. Flip Wilson's $5,000 campaign contribution was one of the largest donations that her campaign ever saw, and while impactful, it was a drop in the bucket compared to her primary opponents. She did not have the support of most of her Black male Democratic colleagues in Congress, or other political leaders at the time. They couldn't stand the idea that Chisholm would jump the line to run for president without their permission. She did not have equitable airtime in the media. The press had dismissed her as a spoiler candidate, even though there were twelve white men and one Asian woman also in the race for the Democratic nomination. She did not have the undivided support of the leaders of the feminist movement. They hedged, in hopes of influencing the Democratic platform through the male primary candidates—an effort that, in the end, yielded disappointing results on abortion rights.

Ultimately, Chisholm was able to win twenty-eight delegates during the Democratic primary elections. The twelve additional delegates that Chisholm would have earned from the June 1972 California primary election were blocked at the Democratic National Convention when Democrats voted to maintain the winner-take-all rule. Their primary argument was that a change to the delegate rules would cause more fractures for the Democratic Party, though the convention had recently changed the rules to ensure more women and young people were seated as delegates. In the end, Senator McGovern was awarded the 271 delegates from California and won the 1972 Democratic nomination for the presidency. The Democratic Party banned all winner-take-all primaries after this presidential election cycle.

In spite of these structural challenges, Chisholm *did* leverage an essential element in the long process of shifting power in politics: the chance to demonstrate *proof of concept*. Proof that a forty-eight-year-old Black woman and first-generation American can run for president of the United States of America.

While crisscrossing the country engaging voters and explaining the appeal of her policy ideas, Shirley Chisholm actualized Black people's and women's right to run for the highest office in the land. Voters bore witness to what could be with each of Chisholm's campaign rallies and speeches, and her efforts planted the seeds of a future they had yet to even dream of. She beta-tested the power of coalition building with a multicultural, cross-class motley crew of organizers, activists, young people, and Hollywood's elite. She demonstrated a new, gutsy leadership style that was attractive to Black and brown people, and to young people who demanded more from politicians as they began to fully exercise their rights. Chisholm was daring in her intentions to operate outside of the traditional parameters of presidential politics, and in turn these achievements were the true benchmarks for her success in 1972.

Chisholm was in uncharted territory. The rules established for the white men who ran before her simply did not apply. As a result, her candidacy also highlighted the gaps within the Democratic Party's primary process that required attention and reform. From the aforementioned lawsuit to gain the television airtime that she was legally due, to the call for proportionate distribution of the California delegates, Chisholm's run exposed the barriers to entry into presidential politics for minority groups.

So, what would make for a more perfect political party? In April 1972, that ideal party came to life when Chisholm's Hollywood supporters gathered for the storied Welcome to Hollywood fundraiser. Diahann Carroll opened her home to host it, created a space for the first Black woman running for president, and called in her influential friends and cultural leaders to introduce them all to Chisholm's campaign, and in turn a new vision of possibilities in politics. Each guest represented the essential components of attaining and maintaining power. Flip Wilson made an impactful financial donation. Huey P. Newton attended to shake the hand of the woman on whose behalf the Black Panthers were deploying their organizing power. David Frost knew a newsmaker when he saw one, and served as the party's honorary third host, a supportive partner, and a media man observing history. Berry Gordy swept through the event as a cultural kingmaker supporting his old friend and neighbor, Diahann Carroll. Goldie Hawn was there as the social butterfly signaling feminist awareness even while throwing her full support behind a different candidate. Barbara Lee was the first-time voter and the ever-committed campaign staffer focused on official business. And Lee stumbled upon a lifelong ally in Maxine Waters, alongside whom she carries on Chisholm's legacy. Whether they knew it in the moment or not, this was all part of Chisholm's plan to unify voices of marginalized communities in order to present a comprehensive list of demands to the Democratic Party at the convention.

Months later, on set for the *Meet the Press* special episode from Miami, Florida, Chisholm's presidential campaign was at its end. When she declared, "I have broken the ice," she meant that her campaign had given the nation its first taste of a conscious redistribution of power that would be required to disrupt nearly two centuries of tradition. Chisholm was calling for an equitable reset of cultural and political norms, and a reset of the Democratic Party. She wanted to see it transform into a political force that is rooted in the people and meeting their needs. And the first step of that process, according to Chisholm's pedagogy, was *inculcation*. In the world of twenty-first-century politics, that translates into leveraging the playbook Chisholm has left behind of multicultural coalition building and challenging the norms during every single election cycle until it is no longer shocking to witness the rise and celebration of qualified Black women in leadership roles. Thus, Chisholm expected other women to replicate her model again and again to gain power and access. Of course, following Chisholm's political model is easier said than done as racism, harassment, sexism, and sexualization are all unwavering national undercurrents that compound hurdles against Black women in politics. Chisholm's own community dealt her some personal cuts and bruises that come with these harmful "isms." Still, she persisted as a persona non grata and continued to fight.

An addendum to Chisholm's push for inculcation would be to take on this work with a team of one's most faithful allies, just as she enjoyed the unwavering support of Black and Latina leaders such as Fannie Lou Hamer, Gwendolyn Cherry, and Lupe Anguiano throughout her presidential campaign. Allies can be an enduring source of power for a woman candidate. They serve as champions who will extol her efforts publicly and fortify her spirit in private. They create a sense of community and sisterhood—critical ingredients to enduring the blowback that comes with breaking through political ice.

Today, the Black and brown women who dare to run, win, and lose are all picking up the baton from Shirley Chisholm. Yes—losing elections matters just as much as winning. Each campaign shifts the political narrative, increases investments in the political infrastructure, and expands political possibilities. In Chisholm's case, she knew that her 1972 presidential campaign would be an electoral loss for her, but a public political win for Black women and voters. Losing has been a feature of the impactful careers of fearless women, with a key example being Stacey Abrams, the former minority leader of the Georgia House of Representatives, best-selling author, and two-time candidate for governor of Georgia in 2018 and 2022. Abrams is also a longtime voting rights activist who has combated voter suppression and increased voter registration for more than a decade. During her gubernatorial campaigns, Abrams had the money and the polling, but that was insufficient to overcome racism, sexism, and voter suppression lobbed against her and her constituents. In the 2018 gubernatorial election, Abrams came within 1.4 points, or 54,723 votes, of the sitting Secretary of State Brian Kemp. That race was unique as Kemp was formally responsible for running free and fair elections in the state, but he also perpetuated voter suppression efforts when he began to close polling places, and cancel the voter registration of more than 1 million Georgia voters as early as 2012, including 53,000 voters in 2018. As of this writing, not a single state in the United States has ever elected a Black woman to serve as governor. Nonetheless, Abrams' organizing efforts helped establish the conditions for Democrats to compete and win in the South, including winning Georgia in the 2020 presidential election, electing two Democratic senators in 2021, and creating a voter activation playbook for other states in the region.

As more Black women run for office, the Democratic Party is being charged to recognize the value of Black women—our shared ideals, our ability to create impact, and our deep understanding of what the American people urgently need. Even President Biden declared, during his 2020 victory speech, that Black women have "always had his back," and are the driving force within the Democratic Party. But while the president and the party understand that Black women comprise the core of their base and consistently vote for Democrats at rates exceeding 90 percent in repeated election cycles, they have yet to demonstrate a comparable history of supporting Black women's bids for public office. In 2022, after recruiting Justice Cheri Beasley, the first Black woman chief justice of the North Carolina Supreme Court, to run for the US Senate, the Democratic National Committee failed to deliver promised investments to her campaign. Technically, Beasley's campaign outraised her opponent by more than $18 million; however, her fundraising advantage was neutralized by outside spending from Republican-run PACs that invested millions in running negative ads about Beasley's legal judgments and rulings. Moreover, she was combating historic voter trends in the large rural portions of the state, where voters overwhelmingly supported Republican white male candidates in the Senate elections in 2016, 2020, and 2022 by margins of 25–60 percent. Without additional resources, there was no way for her campaign to overcome the lack of political infrastructure in the state, which is one of the investments that "never materialize[d]" from the Democratic National Committee. Those critical resources could have been utilized to organize voters, especially Black and brown voters in rural communities outside of college towns. She also would have benefited from additional investments in ads to correct and counteract the negative narratives promoted by Republicans. Ultimately, Beasley's campaign struggled to create the expansive coalition needed to win the purple state, and she lost the race by 3.2 points, or more than 120,000 votes. This particular midterm election cycle was also remarkable because there were no Black women serving in the US Senate at the time, and the gaping hole in leadership was embarrassingly large.

In spite of the continual efforts of the Black and brown women who compete for these federal seats, as of 2023, only three Black women have ever served in the US Senate (Carol Moseley Braun of Illinois, Kamala Harris of California, and Laphonza Butler of California), and only 106 women of color have ever been elected to Congress in its two and a half centuries of existence. Considering that there are 535 seats to fill each Congress every two years, the proportion demonstrates the national gap in understanding and accepting that Black women are capable leaders. Shirley Chisholm called out this gap decades ago with her three-step prescription: inculcation, reorientation, and education. First, *inculcation* through the repeated campaigns and declarations of Black women's abilities to normalize the reality that Black women are more than capable of running intentional, serious political campaigns. Then, *reorientation* to prompt a shift in the public's biased thinking about, and knee-jerk reactions to, Black women candidates. Instead of immediately dismissing them, voters should pause to learn about their perspectives, values, and policy priorities. Instead of immediately relegating a Black woman's appeal to exclusively Black and brown people, assess her candidacy against the same criteria for leadership as any other candidate. Compare her skills, her policy ideas, and her experience side by side with her competitor. And voters should not only consider how her proposals could address their needs and improve their day-to-day lives, but also speak up about what those needs are. And as noted by Cheri Beasley's 2022 campaign for the US Senate, the Democratic Party could certainly stand to reorient itself to even the playing field and prioritize long-term investments in developing the grassroots infrastructure and operations before attempting to insert a Black woman candidate into a campaign with insufficient support.

And then there's the all-important media. While Shirley Chisholm was shut out from televised debates and discussions during the 1972 Democratic primary election by network executives, today, the media welcomes Black women leaders. But even though visibility is at a higher level, the media maintains a tendency to misunderstand their culture or assign them sexist roles. Vice President Kamala Harris, the first Black person, the first South Asian person, the first woman, and the first HBCU graduate to serve as vice president, has experienced these harmful interactions at every stage of her political ascent—from the campaign trail to the White House. In April 2024, actress and talk show host Drew Barrymore turned to Harris on the plush cream couch on the set of *The Drew Barrymore Show* and, with a shaky, yet overly familiar tone, said to the vice president, "I've been thinking that we really all need a tremendous hug in the world right now. But in our country, we need you to be 'Mom-ala' of the country," a play on "mom" and "Kamala." With all of her grace and poise, the vice president smiled, nodded, and pivoted the conversation toward the strength that tends to go dismissed in women leaders. However, the irony of a wealthy white woman actress and daytime television host turning to the second-most powerful political leader in the nation and asking her to be a mother figure is profoundly misguided. With this reductive request, Barrymore and her audience (which broke into enthusiastic applause) dismissed the centuries of forced servitude that demanded that Black women in America serve as involuntary mother figures to white people and white children. Barrymore's comments conjured images of Black women as mammies charged with caring for the white children of their enslavers. That is not the role of the vice president. And it's safe to assume that if Harris were a man, then Barrymore wouldn't have even considered expressing the thought.

What is needed to counter the over-familiarity, under-estimation, and disrespect aimed at Black women leaders is *education*, the third condition of making political gains for Black women candidates that Chisholm emphasized during the special edition of *Meet the Press* in July 1972. Given Chisholm's extensive training and experience as a teacher, and her master's degree in education from Columbia University's Teachers College, when she said education was necessary, she quite literally meant a quality kindergarten-through-twelfth-grade education, as well as access to ample resources and information for all voters in the nation. Chisholm always saw education as a tool for building awareness, and for facilitating change. As bell hooks wrote, "Our struggle is also a struggle of memory against forgetting," and this concept of education applies to politics and historical context. Remembering our past failings and successes as a nation is central to our collective ability to move forward and drive change without repeating mistakes. This is why Chisholm told every child she met, from middle-schoolers visiting the Capitol Building, to pregnant teens earning their high school diplomas in Brooklyn, "Prioritize your education." It is a tool to understand systems so that they may change them.

Unfortunately, gathering this essential knowledge is exponentially more difficult for everyone when structural barriers impede our collective access. From extremist bans on teaching accurate history in schools, to bans on books written by Black and brown and LGBTQ+ authors, this intentional effort to stymie information is a threat to us all. Not only are bans on information one of the signature traits of fascism, as we've repeatedly witnessed throughout history, but they are also a tool that forces entire communities to forget so that others may rewrite history. To make matters worse, the use of misinformation in politics has been a destabilizing force in our democracy. In 2020 alone, 72 percent of US adults stated that they saw news about the 2020 election that seemed completely false. And the public confusion that results from extremist candidates presenting lies as facts, artificial intelligence being weaponized to misdirect voters, and the public's inability to identify the truth in the digital information age creates a compounding challenge for the nation. Chisholm would undoubtedly reemphasize the critical importance of education as a method of equipping the public with the media literacy and critical thinking skills required to identify authentic sources. Her focus on education is a reminder that the state of the public's awareness and understanding is directly correlated to the health, and survival, of our democracy.

More than fifty years later, Shirley Chisholm's ability to break the ice and prescribe a proactive pathway forward for US politics has informed new generations of Black women reaching for substantive new heights in politics. Chisholm would surely celebrate leaders like Representative Ayanna Pressley who are wielding their power for the people. Those fighting to protect our most basic rights and freedoms, like Stacey Abrams. And those who are creating new ways to empower voters, like Cori Bush. She'd also be overjoyed at the prospect that multiple capable, progressive Black women like Prince George's County Executive Angela Alsobrooks of Maryland and Representative Lisa Blunt Rochester of Delaware could become the fourth and fifth Black women to serve in the US Senate. These leaders are an extension of Chisholm's legacy, and further proof that she succeeded in her effort to be a catalyst for change. Her fingerprints are visible in their ethos, and mark their willingness to fight with, and for, the people.

When melding Chisholm's continued impact with the Democratic Party, party leaders must apply the three steps of inculcation, reorientation, and education in order to better engage and elect Black and brown women candidates. Ideally, sustained investments in coalition building among marginalized communities will lead to a more robust grassroots infrastructure that is primed to yield better electoral success. Additionally, a more robust education and understanding of the difficulties facing Black women candidates should prompt an increased likelihood of follow-through on party commitments. The road map is clear and applicable to current challenges, thanks to Shirley Chisholm. It's just a question of willingness to reorient the party in order to survive.

CONCLUSION

THE POWER

"Everything now, we must assume, is in our hands; we have no right to assume otherwise."

—JAMES BALDWIN, *THE FIRE NEXT TIME*

When the producers for MSNBC's *The Beat* with Ari Melber signaled to me that we were going live to cover breaking news in the 2020 presidential election cycle, I took a deep breath to steady myself as adrenaline pumped through my veins. I was ready to go. Due to COVID-19 precautions, my living room and dining area had become my studio, and my ring light and cell phone were my only pieces of "equipment"—a massive downgrade from the well-lit, multi-camera set full of producers that I was used to. But the minimalist tech was the farthest thing from my mind that afternoon in August 2020. Joe Biden had officially selected his vice presidential nominee. While the campaign hadn't shared the name publicly yet, a close friend messaged me that then-Senator Kamala Harris would be Biden's running mate. "FINALLY," I texted back.

A Black and South Asian woman, and a US Senator who had demonstrated political aptitude and leadership capabilities for fifteen-plus years at the highest levels of government was about to break the centuries-long tradition of white male vice presidents. As Joe Biden's running mate, Harris would be able to connect to Black and brown voters, women voters, and younger voters in a substantive, relatable way that he could not—through her personal experiences as the daughter of immigrants, and as a graduate of a historically Black university. Moreover, a Black woman was finally being recognized as an essential political leader within the Democratic Party. It was long overdue, as Black women have consistently supported Democrats since gaining increased access to the polls with the passage of the Voting Rights Act of 1965.

Immediately, I started reviewing my mental log of all of Harris' political achievements, her political value as part of the 2020 Democratic ticket, and yes, her political liabilities. There were layers to Harris' career thus far, some of which demonstrated her evolution as a leader, and others that were explicit points of criticism during the 2020 Democratic primary election. Harris had been a forward-thinking leader who called for marriage equality as a district attorney, having married some of the first same-sex couples in San Francisco to receive a marriage license on Valentine's Day in 2004 after the city declared same-sex marriage legal. As California's attorney general, Harris filed briefs opposing anti-trans bathroom bills, she ended the "panic" defense in criminal trials, and she established the Bureau of Children's Justice to protect kids from abuse and assault.

As a prosecutor, Harris opposed the death penalty, and championed diversion programs for young people charged with low-level drug offenses. She also fostered a powerful reputation for not suffering fools as a US senator who methodically questioned Supreme Court nominees like Brett Kavanaugh in 2018, prompting his visible discomfort. The image of a Black woman in power making a white man (who was being considered for a lifetime appointment to the highest court in the land) sweat and stumble over his words was striking. It upset then-President Donald Trump so deeply that he described Harris as being "extraordinarily nasty."

Conversely, there were negative components in her previous roles that were flagged during the 2020 Democratic presidential primary, including that Harris had enforced bans on gender-affirming care to incarcerated trans people, and that she implemented an anti-truancy program that threatened parents of students who missed more than thirty days of school with jail time. Overall, Harris' record reflected both promising, human-centered policies as well as some initiatives that were rightfully questioned. While discussing these programs with the press, Harris took responsibility for her office's briefs opposing gender-affirming care for incarcerated trans people during her two terms stating that, "the buck stops with [her]." She also emphasized that the policies conflicted with her personal beliefs. When it came to the truancy initiative, Harris stood by the efficacy of the program, and highlighted how infrequent prosecution against parents occurred as school interventions take place long before the attorney general's office is engaged.

Equipped with my analysis, I was prepared to recognize the excitement, and the realities, of Harris' nomination. The live segment on MSNBC reached a fever pitch when Senator Cory Booker of New Jersey referenced the film *Waiting to Exhale* to describe the moment we were witnessing. He explained that the announcement was an opportunity for Black women in the Democratic Party to exhale, literally and figuratively, and appreciate the party's acknowledgment of Black women's power. I snapped my fingers and nodded my head in agreement as he spoke. When Melber directed his next follow-up question to me, I remarked how extremely refreshing it was to see a Black man celebrating and supporting a Black woman as she ascended, and I asked Senator Booker to bring more Black men along with him. Black men's engagement and support of Harris was a marked transition from what Congresswoman Shirley Chisholm had experienced from her Black male Democratic colleagues in the early 1970s. Booker, Melber, and the other panelists were tickled by my direct tone and invitation, and we shared our appreciation for each other and the moment. History was being made, and not only did I have a front row seat, but I also had the privilege of analyzing it in real time on-air.

My segment covering Kamala Harris' historic vice presidential nomination brings to mind a separate noteworthy on-air moment during *The David Frost Show* in 1969. While conversing on the vibrant orange, maroon, and purple set, David Frost asked Shirley Chisholm, "Do you think there can ever be a woman President of the United States?" Without hesitation, Chisholm affirmed the notion by stating, "Oh, yes, yes. It's coming." Through her signature tone of clarity and intention, she conveyed an inevitability that went beyond what Frost and the live audience could imagine for the future of the United States.

Clearly bowled over, Frost blurted out, "When? Where?" Chisholm remained grounded and steady as she predicted that the first woman president would be elected "in about 70 or 75 years." She also stated two critical conditions that voters would have to satisfy in order for the political aspiration to be attainable: first, that women and young people unite, and second, that men step aside.

Chisholm predicted all of this before she ever considered running for president, and her conditions were an extension of her belief that "women and students will save this nation." That unwavering belief was likely rooted in her awareness of her own power, and her experiences as a teacher pouring into children and young people who demonstrated unadulterated promise and fearlessly questioned everything around them. Still, even under the timeline that Chisholm predicted, her own presidential campaign was seventy-two years ahead of schedule.

Premature as it was, Chisholm's courageous bid began to soften the calcified political environment that was resistant to the notion of a woman president, no less a Black woman president. The two primary strategies of her campaign were power building with marginalized communities, and directly challenging men's presumed right to lead. Both components aligned with what she had laid out on *The David Frost Show* three years before.

When it came to tapping into the power of women and young people, she understood that these two communities would need to unite and consolidate their political power "in spite of racial differences, class differences, [and] economic differences." That unity would supercharge the power of women, who comprise 50.4 percent of the country's population, and the people who are set to inherit the nation and all of its problems. However, the biggest hurdles to achieving this unity include the enduring strength of white supremacy, internalized sexism, and capitalism. In 1972, and today, these factors present as white women who hedge, and are unable to fully support a woman candidate, white women who feel more aligned with racist leaders (including the 47 percent and 53 percent of white women who voted for Donald Trump in 2016 and 2020, respectively), and young people who were disaffected and turned off from engaging in politics altogether because current leaders were demonstrably ineffective at addressing their concerns.

While this gulf is not insurmountable, it will require a dynamic candidate who can appeal to, and mobilize, large swaths of both demographic groups, just as Barack Obama did in 2008 and 2012. Obama's presidential campaigns inspired hope in women and young millennials to the degree that they were willing to unite and deliver a decisive electoral win for the first Black president of the United States.

On the other explicit condition of men stepping aside, Chisholm believed that a timeline of seventy-plus years would give "gentlemen a chance to get acclimated for the thing that is to happen in the future, because it is going to happen." Chisholm cut to the chase: Men are not the answer to our collective challenges, and the sooner they accept it, the sooner we all accept it, the better off we will all be. Men have had centuries to do their worst leading this nation, and they certainly did just that. They established foundational wealth in a capitalist system powered by the unpaid labor of kidnapped, enslaved people, and that very system is currently powered by laborers who are merely trying to survive. They did their worst with their enduring efforts to control women by way of constitutional laws that were written with the explicit purpose of restricting them from voting and having bodily autonomy, similar to laws restricting women today. And over the course of centuries, they perpetually refused to respond to the needs of bleeding people—whether those people are victims of gun violence, menstruating people, or global communities who've experienced US-funded munitions demolishing their homes and their people.

During Chisholm's campaign, she confronted Black men who openly mocked and minimized her run, and she successfully challenged the white media executives and candidates who attempted to ignore her entirely. Today, there have been few examples of men stepping aside so that women can claim political power—but 2024 yielded the biggest opportunity yet.

In the summer of 2024, President Joe Biden left the presidential race and passed the political torch to his running mate, Vice President Kamala Harris.

On the heels of a disappointing debate performance against Donald Trump in June, Joe Biden faced pressure from Democrats, publicly and privately, to step aside. While the Democratic National Committee stood firmly behind Biden, fault lines formed among Democratic leaders across the nation. Representatives, senators, and donors called for Biden to step down for the sake of the party's chance to win the November general election. After three weeks of a growing chorus calling on Biden to "pass the torch," he relented and immediately endorsed Vice President Kamala Harris as his successor. The moment President Biden left the race, the campaign's resources, staff, offices, and fundraising haul all passed to Harris; pledged delegates to the Democratic National Convention began discussing their support for Harris' nomination; Democratic leaders across the nation released endorsements one after the other; and voters expressed their support by donating $81 million to the campaign within twenty-four hours of Biden's announcement (breaking fundraising records). The extent of voters' excitement was captured in the fact that 60 percent of the donations were from first-time donors. This signifies that voters who were previously disengaged started locking in and getting active as soon as Vice President Harris moved to the top of the Democratic ticket.

With the endorsements and funds flowing in Harris' direction, she was quickly established as the one to beat for the Democratic nomination for president, and her supporters welcomed her with a warm embrace—the grassroots organization Win with Black Women convened 44,000 Black women digitally in support of Harris' presidential campaign within hours of its launch. The gathering was seen as a validating show of force that signaled to the nation that Black women were wasting no time in aligning behind Harris and organizing on her behalf. That call also set a standard that was quickly duplicated by Black men, white women, Latinas, Asian women, White men, Indigenous people, and Latinos.

The Kamala Harris 2024 presidential campaign was off to a promising start, but it wasn't all support for Harris. Within minutes of Biden's announcement, the Republican Party and racist individuals began attacking Harris' gender, her Blackness, and her leadership abilities. Donald Trump's running mate, JD Vance, US Senator from Ohio, remarked that Harris has only been "collecting a government check for the past 20 years." Vance's flaccid attempt to reduce Harris' decades-long career as vice president, US senator, California attorney general, and San Francisco district attorney to the "lazy, welfare queen" trope was a warm-up act for Republicans.

While Republicans fumed to the media about the Harris campaign, many voters saw opportunity, including myself. I saw an opportunity to realize Shirley Chisholm's goal of electing a woman president of the

United States by following her playbook. Frankly, Harris is starting in a different political plane compared to Chisholm's 1972 campaign, but the playbook for power building still applied, and the Welcome to Hollywood party was the model. The only question is, which role do voters want to play?

They could join Diahann Carroll as a convener. She rolled out the red carpet for Chisholm at a moment when she was confronting detractors on a daily basis, and she validated the campaign by lending her national celebrity to the effort. Carroll's support demonstrated the power of Black women joining forces in positive, impactful ways. Voters could mirror Flip Wilson and put their money where their mouth is. Wilson's contribution was inspired by Chisholm's commitment to returning power to the people, and he also supported Chisholm's mission of driving the nation toward a future where his money would be replaced by publicly funded campaigns, and the power of the super-rich would be neutralized.

Voters who are interested in establishing community connections could opt to follow Huey P. Newton's lead and challenge power structures from within the system, by mobilizing others. There's also Barbara Lee, who was a politically disengaged young person—that is, until she met Shirley Chisholm, a leader who inspired her to action. Lee was also a highly effective strategist who identified connections between organizations with similar goals, and successfully fostered new, substantive relationships.

When it comes to communications, there is always a need for supporters who are willing to combat misinformation with receipts and evidence, and to amplify candidates of their choice, in person and online. Human-centered information sharing, similar to David Frost's approach, is critical to building community, and maintaining the health of our democracy.

It's also important to be prepared to challenge those closest to us, in addition to strangers on the internet. Just as Diahann Carroll introduced Berry Gordy to Shirley Chisholm's campaign, she pushed her friend to expand his thinking in a safe, welcoming way. She also reminded him that just because he was a music mogul, that did not mean that he knew everything. Goldie Hawn was also encouraged to learn more about Chisholm at the Welcome to Hollywood party; taking the time to listen and learn, even if you're not ultimately bought in, makes for better-informed voters.

There's a role for everyone to play. It's simply a question of how each of us will respond when met with opportunity. Shirley Chisholm chose to take as much into her own two hands as possible because she understood the recipe for change all along. And she repeatedly attempted to show and tell the nation the solution, in spite of being dismissed and targeted as a source of consternation.

Today, the question remains whether or not this nation can meet the conditions that Chisholm modeled and outlined by 2044 or even sooner. And whether or not this nation is willing to make the changes required to unite and return power to the people. To be clear, Shirley Chisholm never promised perfection, but what she did propose was a better way to exist, and she empowered people to grab on to those possibilities with everything that they had.

We have all been invited to the party. It's now just a matter of showing up.

BIBLIOGRAPHY AND SOURCES

General Reference

Carroll, D. (2008). *The Legs Are the Last to Go: Aging, Acting, Marrying, and Other Things I Learned the Hard Way.* HarperCollins.

Carroll, D., and R. Firestone. (1986). *Diahann: An Autobiography.* Little, Brown and Co.

Chisholm, S. (1970). *Unbought and Unbossed.* Houghton Mifflin Harcourt.

Chisholm, S. (1973). *The Good Fight.* HarperCollins.

Curwood, A. C. (2022). *Shirley Chisholm: Champion of Black Feminist Power Politics.* University of North Carolina Press.

Gordy, B. (2013). *To Be Loved: The Music, the Magic, the Memories of Motown.* Grand Central Publishing.

Lee, B. (2006). *Renegade for Peace and Justice: Congresswoman Barbara Lee Speaks for Me.* Rowman & Littlefield.

Lynch, S., Director. (2004). *Chisholm '72—Unbought & Unbossed.* [Documentary film.]

Newton, H. P. (1973). *Revolutionary Suicide.* Harcourt Brace Jovanovich.

Whitaker, M. (2023). *Saying It Loud: 1966—The Year Black Power Challenged the Civil Rights Movement.* Simon & Schuster.

Chapter One: The Party

AP Wire. (1957). "New Home of Lance Reventlow for His 21st Birthday." [Press photo.]

Balcaen III, R. (2022). *Raoul 'Sonny' Balcaen.* Evro Publishing.

Carroll, D. (2008). *The Legs Are the Last to Go: Aging, Acting, Marrying, and Other Things I Learned the Hard Way.* HarperCollins.

Carroll, D., and R. Firestone. (1986). *Diahann: An Autobiography.* Little, Brown and Co.

Chisholm, S. (1970). *Unbought and Unbossed.* Houghton Mifflin Harcourt.

Chisholm, S. (1969, March 26). "Remarks on an Appraisal of the Conflict in Vietnam." Congressional Record 115, p. H7765.

Coleman, H., Interviewer. (1998, March 3). "Diahann Carroll Interview." [Video.] Television Academy Foundation.

Curwood, A. C. (2022). *Shirley Chisholm: Champion of Black Feminist Power Politics.* University of North Carolina Press.

Television Academy Foundation. (2011, January 20). "Diahann Carroll Discusses Dynasty." [Video]. *YouTube.*

"Find Someone Who Can Hear the People Cry—The Black Panther Party Endorses Sister Shirley Chisholm for US President." (1972, May 6). *The Black Panther,* Volume 8 Number 7.

1st Dist. Citizens for Chisholm. (1972). "To Vote March 21st for Shirley Chisholm." [Press release].

Haber, J. (1972, March 13). "Shirley Chisholm Supporter." *Los Angeles Times.*

Lynch, S. (2003). "Interview with Barbara Lee." Brooklyn College Special Collections, Box 10.

"Mrs. Chisholm Names Aide." (1972, April 4). *New York Times.*

"New Lady in Town." (1984, May 2). *Dynasty.* Season 4, Episode 26.

Scheader, C. (1990). *Shirley Chisholm, Teacher and Congresswoman.* Enslow Publishing.

Schochet, L. (2019). "The Child Care Crisis Is Keeping Women Out of the Workforce." Center for American Progress.

Starr, H. (2014, September 1). "New York Illustrated: The Irrepressible Shirley Chisholm." 1969 NBC News Special. [Video]. *YouTube.*

"Top in the News." (1972, May 4). *Southwest News.*

"24 Million Americans—Poverty in the United States: 1969" (1970). No. P60-76. United States Census Bureau.

The National Visionary Leadership Project. (2010, April 7). "Shirley Chisholm: Growing Up in Barbados." [Video]. *YouTube.*

"Want to Grow the Economy? Fix the Child Care Crisis." (2019). Council for a Strong America.

Weil, R. (1974, December). "Diahann Carroll: I Just Have to Be Home for Christmas." *House Beautiful.*

Chapter Two: The Money

Anderson, N. (1972, May 31). "Who Stars Want for President." *San Francisco Examiner.*

Ayesh, R. (2019, May 15). "Harris: Biden Would Make a 'Great' Vice Presidential Running Mate." *Axios.*

Cadelago, C. (2019, May 15). "'It's Infuriating': Kamala Harris Team Galled by Biden Veep Talk." *Politico.*

"Campaign Finance Reports Contain Fascinating, Puzzling Data." (1972, June 20). *Sacramento Bee.*

Chisholm, S. (1970). *Unbought and Unbossed.* Houghton Mifflin Harcourt.

Chisholm, S. (1973). *The Good Fight.* HarperCollins.

Citizens United v. Federal Election Commission. (2010). Supreme Court of the United States.

Cook, K. (2013). *Flip: The Inside Story of TV's First Black Superstar.* Penguin.

Sullivan, E. (1972, April 14). "Little Old New York." *Daily News.*

Detrow, S., and A. Khalid. (2019, December 3). "Kamala Harris Drops Out of Presidential Race." NPR.

Evers-Hillstrom, K. (2020). "More Money, Less Transparency: A Decade Under Citizens United." *OpenSecrets.*

Feddoes, S. (1972, March 4). "Please Be Seated." *NY Amsterdam News.*

Flamini, R. (1972, January 31). "When You're Hot, You're Hot." *Time.*

Fuchs, H., and C. Cameron. (2023, August 14). "Listen to Trump Pressure an Official to 'Find' Enough Votes for Him to Win Georgia." *New York Times.*

Greenfeld, J. (1971, November 14). "Flip Wilson: 'My Life Is My Own.'" *New York Times.*

Haber, J. (1974, November 24). "The Flip Side of Clerow Wilson." *Los Angeles Times.*

"How Trump's Trials for 91 Felony Charges in 4 States Could Take Over His Campaign." (2024, February 22). NPR.

Johnson, T. (1972, January 27). "Head of Operation Breadbasket Says He Opposes Mrs. Chisholm." *New York Times.*

Johnson, T. (2023, December 10). "Joe Biden's Los Angeles Fundraising Swing Brings in More Than $15 Million, Jeffrey Katzenberg Says." *Deadline.*

Kapur, S. (2023, May 17). "Trump: 'I Was Able to Kill Roe v. Wade.'" NBC News.

Lesher, S. (1972, June 25). "The Short, Unhappy Life of Black Presidential Politics, 1972." *New York Times.*

Levinthal, D. (2020, August 26). "Meet the GOP's Biggest Hollywood Donors." *Business Insider.*

Lynch, S. (2003). "Interview with Arlie Scott." Brooklyn College Special Collections, Box 10, tape 1 of 2.

"McGovern Calls for Tax Reform." (1972, January). *New York Times.*

"McGovern Voting Record—Military Appropriations 1966–1970."

"Presidential Candidate Data Summary Tables." (2008). Federal Election Commission.

"Presidential Pre-Nomination Campaign Receipts Through December 31, 2019." (2020). Federal Election Commission.

"'72 Election Set Spending Record." (1976, April 25). *New York Times.*

"Sound Motive, Dubious Method." (1970, August 31). *New York Times.*

"State Vote." (1972, June 7). *Santa Maria Times.*

"The Flip Wilson Show—Jan 21, 1971—Geraldine and Muhammad Ali." (2019, January 14). [Video]. *YouTube.*

"The Flip Wilson Show—Feb 18, 1971—Geraldine and David Frost." (2024, March 23). [Video]. *YouTube.*

"The McGovern-Hatfield Amendment to End the War—Additional CoSponsor." (1970). Congressional Record—Senate.

"TV's First Black Superstar." (1972, January 31). *Time.*

"2008 Electoral College Results." (n.d.). National Archives.

Weissert, W. (2023, December 9). "President Biden Fundraising in Hollywood with Strikes Over." AP News.

Whack, E. H. (2019, July 8). "AP Interview: Kamala Harris on Race and Electability in 2020." AP News.

Wu-Tang Clan. (1993). *"C.R.E.A.M."* Universal Music.

Chapter Three: The Activist

AP Archive. (1972, June 12). "Shirley Chisholm Campaigns in New York." [Video]. *YouTube.*

Bell, P. (n.d.). *Public Trust in Government: 1958–2024.* Pew Research Center.

"Black Confab Leaves Main Job Unfinished." (1972, March 13). *The Times.*

"Blacks Favor Chisholm, Hatcher Says." (1972, March 12). *The Times.*

Booker, S. (1972, February 17). "Ticker Tape U.S.A." *Jet.*

Booker, S. (1972, March 30). "Black Political Convention Is Successful Despite Splits and Tactical Differences." *Jet.*

Brooks, A. (2018, September 12). "'The District Has Changed': How Ayanna Pressley Won the 7th." WBUR.

Brown, E. (1992). *A Taste of Power: A Black Woman's Story.* Pantheon.

Buckley, T. (1972, March 24). "Mrs. Chisholm Finds District Leaders in Opposing Camp." *New York Times.*

"California Poll Puts McGovern Far in the Lead." (1972, June 3). *Palm Beach Post.*

"Statement of Vote—Historical Voter Registration and Participation in Statewide General Elections 1910–2008." (2000) California Secretary of State.

Carroll, D. (2008). *The Legs Are the Last to Go: Aging, Acting, Marrying, and Other Things I Learned the Hard Way.* HarperCollins.

Chisholm, S. (1970). *Unbought and Unbossed.* Houghton Mifflin Harcourt.

Curwood, A. C. (2022). *Shirley Chisholm: Champion of Black Feminist Power Politics.* University of North Carolina Press.

Dezenski, L. (2018, May 18). "CBC Endorses Capuano in Massachusetts Democratic Primary." *Politico.*

Evans, N. (1966, August 8). "The Tragedy of Black Power." *Los Angeles Times.*

"Have the Black Panthers Really Changed at All?" (1972, March 7). *Indiana Gazette.*

"Hoover Calls Panthers No. 1 U.S. Danger." (1969, July 15). *Chicago Tribune.*

"Huey Percy Newton." (1972, February 12). *National Observer.*

"Huey Percy Newton File." Federal Bureau of Investigation. #HQ 105-165429.

Johnson, T. (1972, January 27). "Head of Operation Breadbasket Says He Opposes Mrs. Chisholm." *New York Times.*

Kifner, J. (1976, May 9). "F.B.I. Sought Doom of Panther Party." *New York Times.*

Lacy, A. (2019, March 22). "House Democratic Leadership Warns It Will Cut Off Any Firms That Challenge Incumbents." *The Intercept.*

Lesher, S. (1972, June 25). "The Short, Unhappy Life of Black Presidential Politics, 1972." *New York Times.*

"Life and Career of Shirley Chisholm." (1993, February 28). [Video]. C-SPAN.

Lynch, S. (2003). "Interview with Bobby Seale." Brooklyn College Special Collections, Box 10.

Lynch, S. (2003). "Interview with Representative Barbara Lee." Brooklyn College Special Collections, Box 10.

"New Pendleton Unit to Aid Viet Force." (1966, August 1). *Los Angeles Times.*

Newton, H. P. (1973). *Revolutionary Suicide.* Harcourt Brace Jovanovich.

"NY Views on Vietnam Cover Wide Spectrum." (1966, August 1). *Los Angeles Times.*

"Panthers Endorse Shirley Chisholm." (1972, April 28). *San Bernardino County Sun.*

Quilantan, B., and D. Cohen. (2017, July 14). "Trump Tells Dem Congresswomen: Go Back Where You Came From." *Politico.*

Russonello, G. (2021, March 9; updated 2021, March 31). "The D.C.C.C. Blacklist Is No More." *New York Times.*

Signal Boost. (2022, February 18). "Interview with Representative Barbara Lee." *SiriusXM Progress.*

The Black Panther. (1972, May 6). Vol. 8, Nos. 7–9.

The Extent of Poverty in the United States: 1959 to 1966. (1968). US Bureau of the Census. Current Population Reports. Series P-20, No. 54.

The History Makers. (2021, April 6). "An Evening with Diahann Carroll (Washington, D.C. 2005)." [Video].

Tolliver, J. (2023, September 9). "Interview with Representative Barbara Lee."

Turner, W. (1972, June 7). "Humphrey Loses." *New York Times.*

Werbeck, N. (2018, September 5). "'Nothing Was Off Limits': Intimate Photos from Ayanna Pressley's Campaign." NPR.

Whitaker, M. (2023). *Saying It Loud: 1966—The Year Black Power Challenged the Civil Rights Movement.* Simon & Schuster.

Chapter Four: The Youth

Brockell, G. (2021, August 18). "She Was the Only Member of Congress to Vote Against War in Afghanistan. Some Called Her a Traitor." *Washington Post.*

Chisholm, S. (1969, March 26). "Remarks on an Appraisal of the Conflict in Vietnam." *Congressional Record*, 115.

Chisholm, S. (1970). *Unbought and Unbossed.* Houghton Mifflin Harcourt.

Chisholm, S. (1973). *The Good Fight.* HarperCollins.

"Civilian Unemployment Rate, 1964–2010." (n.d.). Department of Labor, Bureau of Labor Statistics.

"Democratic Presidential Primary: Pennsylvania 2024." (n.d.). CNN.

Gorry, C., and AP Photo. (1969, March 26). "Rep. Shirley Chisholm (D-N.Y.) Poses on the Steps of the Capitol in Washington." [Press photo].

Hamas. (2022). Office of the Director of National Intelligence.

Hezakya Newz & Films. (2022, July 9). "1969 Special Report: 'The Irrepressible Shirley Chisholm.'" [Video]. *YouTube.*

Hickling, L. (1969, March 27). "16 House Democrats Urge U.S. End War." *Press & Sun-Bulletin.*

Horton, A. (2021, April 15). "D.C. Guard Misused Helicopters in Low-Flying Confrontation with George Floyd Protesters, Army Concludes." *Washington Post.*

"Israel Tells Gazans to Move South or Risk Being Seen as 'Terrorist' Partner." (2023, October 22). Reuters.

"Israel, Hamas at War: Latest Updates." (2023, October 12). Reuters.

Kennedy, R. F. (1968, April 4). "Kennedy Speech—Indianapolis."

Khurana, M. (2024, May 8). "How These University of Texas-Austin Students View Gaza War Protests on Their Campus." WSKG.

King Jr., M. L. (1968, April 3). "I've Been to the Mountaintop."

Lewis, J., and T. Hensley, (n.d.). *The May 4 Shootings at Kent State University: The Search for Historical Accuracy.* Kent State University.

"LIVE UPDATES: Pro-Palestine Protesters Begin Encampment in Harvard Yard." (2024, April 25). *Harvard Crimson.*

McEvoy, O. (2024). "Annual Number of United States Military Personnel Conscripted Via the Draft from 1964 to 1973." *Statista.*

"Michigan Election Results and Maps 2020." (n.d.). CNN.

"Michigan Presidential Primary Results 2024." (n.d.). AP News.

Moore, E. (2024, March 6). "'Uncommitted' Movement Spreads to Super Tuesday States." NPR.

Nichols, J. (2024, March 8). "The 'Uncommitted' Movement Keeps Getting Stronger." *The Nation.*

Office of the Surgeon General. (2024, June 17). *Social Media and Youth Mental Health.* HHS.gov.

"Pennsylvania Presidential Results 2020." (2020). *Politico.*

Poverty Increases by 1.2 Million in 1970. (1971). US Department of Commerce, Bureau of the Census. Series P-60, No. 77.

Robinson, K. (2024, April 18). "What Is Hamas?" Council on Foreign Relations.

Rogers, K., and M. Radcliffe. (2023, May 25). "Over 100 Anti-LGBTQ+ Laws Passed in the Last Five Years—Half of Them This Year." *FiveThirtyEight.*

Signal Boost. (2022, February 18). "Interview with Representative Barbara Lee." *SiriusXM Progress.*

"The Youth Vote." (1972, August 21). *New York Times.*

"34,735 Palestinians Killed and 78,108 Injured in Israel's Military Offensive on Gaza Since Oct.7—Gaza Health Ministry." (2024, May 6). Reuters.

Tolliver, J. (2023, September 9). "Interview with Representative Barbara Lee."

Uncommitted National Movement. https://www.uncommittedmovement.com/.

US Constitution, Amendment XXVI.

"Vietnam War U.S. Military Fatal Casualty Statistics." (2008). National Archives.

Vietnam: 1965–1975. (2015). World Peace Foundation.

"Voting Laws Roundup: December 2022." (n.d.). Brennan Center for Justice.

"Voting Laws Roundup: October 2021." (2021, July 22). Brennan Center for Justice.

"Voting Laws Roundup: October 2023." (n.d.). Brennan Center for Justice.

"Where College Protesters Have Been Arrested or Detained." (2024, June 17). *New York Times.*

"Wisconsin Presidential Results 2020." (n.d.). *Politico.*

"Wisconsin Primary Election Results 2024." (2024, May 31). *New York Times.*

Chapter Five: The Media

"About Ms. Magazine." (2023, November 1). *Ms.*

Ali, S. S. (2020, September 27). "'Not by Accident': False 'Thug' Narratives Have Long Been Used to Discredit Civil Rights Movements." NBC News.

"Black Americans' Experiences with News." (n.d.). Pew Research.

Bundel, A. (2019, July 18). "Television Made the Apollo 11 Moon Landing a Moment of National Unity." NBC News.

Carroll, D., and R. Firestone. (1986). *Diahann: An Autobiography.* Little, Brown and Co.

Carter's Remasters. (2024, January 15). "John & Yoko on 'The David Frost Show' 1969." [Video]. *YouTube.*

Chisholm, S. (1970). *Unbought and Unbossed.* Houghton Mifflin Harcourt.

Chisholm, S. (1973). *The Good Fight.* HarperCollins.

Christy, M. (1970, July 31). "Congress' Pepperpot." *Boston Globe.*

Christy, M. (1972, January 9) "Diahann and David: 'An Exquisite One-to-One Relationship.'" *Boston Globe.*

Clifton, D. (2020, August 17). "She's 'Nasty': Trump Deploys the 'Angry Black Woman' Trope Against Kamala Harris." NBC News.

"Concept of Poor as Lazy Disputed." (1972, December 26). *Chicago Tribune.*

"David Frost Replaces Merv Griffin on Afternoon Talk Show." (1969, June 28). *Times Record.*

Day, C. (2020, August 13). "Trump Calls Kamala Harris a 'Madwoman' in Latest Attack on Biden's VP Pick." *Wall Street Journal.*

Frost, D. (1993). *An Autobiography. Part One—From Congregations to Audiences.* HarperCollins.

Gerbner, G., L. Gross, M. Morgan, and N. Signorielli. (n.d.). *Living with Television: The Dynamics of the Cultivation Process.* Annenberg School of Communications—University of Pennsylvania.

Hellman, P. (1969, December 7). "What Makes David Frost Talk." *New York Times Magazine.*

"Huey Newton FBI File" (n.d.). Federal Bureau of Investigation. #HQ 105-165429, Section 13.

"Introducing The 19th: A Nonprofit, Nonpartisan Newsroom to Inform, Engage and Empower America's Women." (2020, January 27). PR Newswire.

Issues and Answers—Episode Transcript. (1972, June 4). ABC.

"Julia May Not Be Single in Real Life." (1970, August 27). *Jet.*

Karni, A., and J. Peters. (2020, August 25). "Her Voice? Her Name? G.O.P.'s Raw Personal Attacks on Kamala Harris." *New York Times.*

Kifner, J. (1976, May 9). "F.B.I. Sought Doom of Panther Party." *New York Times.*

Lynch, S., Director. (2004). *Chisholm '72—Unbought & Unbossed.* [Documentary film.]

"McGovern Terms It Illegal for C.B.S. to Exclude Him." (1968, August 17). *New York Times.*

"Mrs. Chisholm Is Pleased." (1972, June 3). *New York Times.*

"19th News. (2024, June 27). "The 19th's Mission, Values and Revenue Model—The 19th." The 19th*.

"Other Actions, All Services." (1972, July 3). *Broadcasting Magazine.*

ReelinInTheYears66. (2016, May 18). "The David Frost Show [1969–1972] Demo." [Video]. *YouTube.*

Scherf, M. (1971, November 17). "Numbers Fall, but Presence Felt." *Boston Globe.*

"Shirley Chisholm Assails Media for 'Deciding' Who Is Frontrunner." (1972, June 5). *Peninsula Times Tribune.*

"Shirley Predicts a Nixon Win." (1972, January 29). *Philadelphia Inquirer.*

Television. (n.d.). Library of Congress. https://guides.loc.gov/american-women-moving-image/television.

The Frost Tapes (2020, October 6). Season 1, Episodes 2–3.

"Trump Stokes 'Birther' Conspiracy Theory About Kamala Harris." (2020, August 14). BBC.

U.S. Census Bureau History: Philo Farnsworth and the Invention of Television. (2023). United States Census Bureau.

"U.S. Court Rules Mrs. Chisholm Must Receive Equal Time on TV." (1972, June 3). *New York Times.*

United States. (1934). Communications Act of 1934.

Chapter Six: The Celebrity Influence

"Americans' Dismal Views of the Nation's Politics." (2023, September 19). Pew Research Center.

BarackObamadotcom. (2012, April 4). "The Story of 'Fired Up! Ready to Go!'—Obama for America 2012." [Video]. *YouTube.*

Bronson, F. (1981). *The Billboard Book of Number One Hits.* Billboard Books.

Bronson, F. (1998, November 7). "The Temptations." *Billboard.* Vol. 110, No. 45.

Cai, S. (2024, June 2). "Guilty Verdict Fuels Trump's Push for Black Voters." *Axios.*

"Campaign Issues and Candidate Positions." (n.d.). ICPSR.

Cannon, G. (1972, May 1). "Motown Making Millions." *Guardian.*

Carroll, D. (2008). *The Legs Are the Last to Go: Aging, Acting, Marrying, and Other Things I Learned the Hard Way.* HarperCollins.

Coleman, C. (2024, February 27). "Fat Joe Explains Why He Had to Buy Donald Trump's New Sneaker." *XXL Magazine.*

Coscarelli, J. (2021, January 20). "Lil Wayne and Kodak Black Among 4 Hip-Hop Figures Trump Pardoned." *New York Times.*

Fung, K. (2024, January 28). "Can Taylor Swift Sway Voting in the 2024 Election." *Newsweek.*

Gaye, M. (1971). *What's Going On.* [Album].

Gordy, B. (2013). *To Be Loved: The Music, the Magic, the Memories of Motown.* Grand Central Publishing.

Gramlich, J. (2021, January 22). "Trump Used His Clemency Power Sparingly Despite a Raft of Late Pardons and Commutations." Pew Research Center.

Haber, J. "Shirley Chisholm Supporter." (1972, March 13). *Los Angeles Times.*

"Inside Motown's Private Meetings." (2013, June 16). [Video]. OWN.

"Julia Lunchbox—For All the World to See." (n.d.). University of Maryland, Baltimore County.

Karni, A., and M. Haberman. (2020, February 4). "Trump and Kushner Saw Super Bowl Ad as Way of Making Inroads with Black Voters." *New York Times.*

Lane, B. (1972, May 25). "People Places 'n' Situwayshuns." *Los Angeles Sentinel.*

Lauer, C., and J. Colvin. (2024, February 17). "Trump Hawks $399 Branded Shoes at 'Sneaker Con,' a Day After a $355 Million Ruling Against Him." AP.

McDougal, D. (2008, January 20). "The Perils of Picking Presidents." *Los Angeles Times.*

"Most in a Poll Term Vietnam a Mistake." (1970, June 28). *New York Times.*

No Strings. 1962 World Premier. (n.d.).

Noble, P. A. (1962). "The Supremes—Where Did Our Love Go." [Video]. *YouTube.*

"Poll: Black Support Helps Clinton Extend Lead." (2003). CNN.
Ribowsky, M. (2010). *Signed, Sealed, and Delivered: The Soulful Journey of Stevie Wonder.* Trade Paper Press.
Ritz, D. (2003). *Divided Soul: The Life of Marvin Gaye.* Da Capo Press.
" 'Skinny Kid with Funny Name' Rallies Democrats." (2004, July 28). NBC News.
Steinhauser, P. (2008). "Poll: Obama Makes Big Gains Among Black Voters." CNN.
"The Most Popular Democrats (Q2 2024)." (2024). YouGov.
Theo Von. (2023, October 3). "Sexyy Red: This Past Weekend w/Theo Von #465." [Video]. *YouTube.*
Tolliver, J. (2024, March). "Interview with Former Surrogate Coordinator."
Turner, B., and G. Turner, Directors. (2019). *Hitsville: The Making of Motown.* [Documentary film.]
"2016, 2018, 2020 and 2022 Voter Demographics, Based on Validated Voters." (2023, July 12). Pew Research Center.
"U.S. Senate: Landmark Legislation: Civil Rights Act of 1875." (2023, August 8).
Urban Hollywood 411. (2019, October 7). "Smokey Robinson and Berry Gordy React to Diahann Carroll's Death." [Video]. *YouTube.*
Vega, T. (2013, January 16). "A Show Makes Friends and History." *New York Times.*
Wang, O. (2011, July 14). "The Strange Sound of Motown's Early Hollywood Years." NPR.
Washington, K. (2023). *Thicker than Water.* Little, Brown Spark.
Wete, B. (2022, April 15). "Marvin Gaye's 30 Top Songs on the Billboard Hot 100." *Billboard.*
What's Going On—Marvin Gaye. (n.d.). Classic Motown.
Wilson, L., Director. (2020). *Miss Americana.* Tremolo Productions.
Zeleny, J. (2007, May 3). "Oprah Endorses Obama." *New York Times.*

Chapter Seven: The (White) Feminists

"A Bunny's Tale"—Gloria Steinem. (1963, June 1). *Show Magazine.*
"An Examination of the 2016 Electoral, Based on Validated Voters." (2018, August 9). Pew Research Center.
Becks, M. (1972, May 8). "Butterfly Wings It." *San Francisco Examiner.*

Carroll, D., and R. Firestone. (1986). *Diahann: An Autobiography.* Little, Brown and Co.

Chisholm, S. (1972, January 25). "Presidential Announcement Speech."

Chisholm, S. (1973). *The Good Fight.* HarperCollins.

Curwood, A. C. (2022). *Shirley Chisholm: Champion of Black Feminist Power Politics.* University of North Carolina Press.

Dismore, D. (2020, January 21). "Today in Feminist History: Gloria Steinem and Shirley Chisholm Take Chicago." *Ms.*

Dobbs v. Jackson Women's Health Organization. 597 U.S. 215 (2022).

"Dream for Women, President Chisholm." (1972, February 14). *New York Times.*

Ebert, R. (1969, December 29). "Cactus Flower Review." *Chicago-Sun Times.*

"EDs Refused to Treat Pregnant Women, Leaving One to Miscarry in a Lobby Restroom." (2024, April 19). AP.

"Feminism: The Second Wave." (2020, June 18). National Women's History Museum.

"Four for McGovern . . . 3/4 for McGovern." (1972, April 15). *Barbra Archives.*

Gambino, L. (2016, February 8). "Female Voters Voice Deep Division Over Hillary Clinton: 'Passion Is Everything.'" *Guardian.*

"Gloria Steinem Aids McGovern's Cause." (1972, February 12). *New York Times.*

"Goldie Hawn—Sammy Davis Jr 60th Anniversary Celebration." (1990, June 3). [Video]. *YouTube.*

"Gwendolyn Sawyer Cherry, Esq." (n.d.). Gwen S. Cherry Black Women Lawyers Association.

hooks, b., and M. Jezer. (1982). *Ain't I a Woman: Black Women and Feminism.* South End Press.

Hudson, K. (2017, April 25). "Goldie Hawn." *Interview Magazine.*

"In Decibels, It's McGovern." (1972, May 6). *San Francisco Examiner.*

Khalid, A. (2016, June 9). "Hillary Clinton Fights to Win Over Her Own Demographic: White Women." NPR.

"King Deals Prince Crowning Blow." (1972, April 18). *Los Angeles Times.*

King Jr., M. L. (1964, October 17). "Something Happening in Mississippi." *New York Amsterdam News.*

"Ku Klux Klan Newspaper Declares Support for Trump." (2016, November 2). Reuters.

"Life and Career of Shirley Chisholm." (1993, February 28). [Video]. C-SPAN.

Lynch, S. "Interview with Shirley Chisholm." CC, Box, 9, Tape 1 of 2.

Lynch, S., Director. (2004). *Chisholm '72—Unbought and Unbossed.* [Documentary film].

"McGovern Reveals Names of California Donors." (1972, April 28). *San Bernardino County Sun.*

"McGovern Winds Up Profitable Campaign Swing in California." (1972, April 7). *Napa Valley Register.*

Neumeister, L. (2024, January 9). "Notorious 'Access Hollywood' Tape to Be Shown at Trump's Defamation Trial Damages Phase Next Week." AP.

"New Hollywood Aura Lights McGovern Dinner." (1972, April 10). *Los Angeles Times.*

Rinaldi, O., and S. Mizelle. (2024, January 11). "Trump Brags About Role in Overturning Roe v. Wade but Urges GOP Caution on Abortion." CBS News.

Robertson, N. (1972, July 15). "Democrats Feel Impact of Women's New Power." *New York Times.*

Roe v. Wade, 410 U.S. 113 (1973).

Saillant, C. (2007, March 19). "Activist's 60-Year Fight for Justice." *Los Angeles Times.*

"Sen. McGovern Shows Savvy." (1972, May 18). *Chicago Tribune.*

"Setting the Stage." (2006, July). National Organization for Women.

"Shirley Makes It Official." (1972, January 26). *Berkeley Gazette.*

Siegel, T. (2023, March 8). "Goldie Hawn on Her Big Oscars Regret, the Death of the Movie Star and Not Retiring from Acting Just Yet." *Variety.*

Steinem, G. (1986). *Outrageous Acts and Everyday Rebellions.* Berkley.

"The 42nd Academy Awards, 1970." (1970, April 7). *Oscars.*

"The Best of Laugh-In, March 2011." (2011, January 9). PBS.

Thompson, H. (1969, December 17). "Cactus Flower" Blooms. *New York Times.*

Chapter Eight: The Sisterhood

Anderson, J. (1965, March 28). "Congresswoman Patsy Mink Tells: Why Women Are Needed in Government." *Boston Globe.*

Anderson, Nick. (2000, January 29). "Grandmothers Lobby Lawmakers." *Los Angeles Times.*

Andrews-Dyer, H., and R. E. Thomas. (2020). *Reclaiming Her Time: The Power of Maxine Waters.* Dey Street Books.

AP Archive. (2015, July 23). "USA: Al Gore Concession Speech" [Video]. *YouTube.*

Associated Press. (2024, May 17). "WATCH: Marjorie Taylor Greene, AOC, Jasmine Crockett Clash at House Hearing." [Video]. *YouTube.*

Billings, E. (2005, June 17). "Democrats Form 'Out of Iraq' Caucus in House." *Roll Call.*

"Blacks' Political Future Tied to Coalition-Building." (1998, May 1). *Oakland Tribune.*

Brownstein, R. (1989, March 5). "The Two Worlds of Maxine Waters: Mastering the Back Rooms of Sacramento, Battling Despair on the Streets of L.A." *Los Angeles Times.*

Bush v. Gore. 531 U.S. 98. (2000).

"Cardis Collins." (n.d.). Archives of Women's Political Communications, Iowa State University.

Cathey, L., and J. DiMartino. (2020, November 5). "Trump Calls for Vote Counting to Stop as Path to Victory Narrows, Biden Urges All to 'Stay Calm.'" ABC News.

"CAWP Fact Sheet: List of Women Candidates—Election 1998." (1998). Center for American Women and Politics; Eagleton Institute of Politics; and Rutgers, The State University of New Jersey.

Chisholm, S. (1970). *Unbought and Unbossed.* Houghton Mifflin Harcourt.

Curwood, A. C. (2022). *Shirley Chisholm: Champion of Black Feminist Power Politics.* University of North Carolina Press.

"Electoral College Ballot Count." (2001, January 6). [Video]. CSPAN.

Epstein, K. (2018, April 9). "The First Congresswoman to Give Birth in Office Was No Stranger to Breaking Boundaries." *Washington Post.*

Fandos, N., and E. Cochrane. (2021, January 7). "After Pro-Trump Mob Storms Capitol, Congress Confirms Biden's Win." *New York Times.*

Filkens, D., and D. Canedy. (2000, November 24). "Protest Influenced Miami-Dade's Decision to Stop Recount." *New York Times.*

"Flashback: The Elian Gonzalez Raid." (2015, April 22). [Video]. NBC News.

Fram, A. (2001, January 7). "It's Official: Congress Taps Bush." *Atlanta Journal Constitution.*

Geiger, A. (2024, April 14). "From the Archives: How the Watergate Crisis Eroded Public Support for Richard Nixon." Pew Research Center.

Gstatler, M. (2018, June 30). "Maxine Waters Responds to Death Threats: 'You Better Shoot Straight.'" *The Hill.*

"House Session: Maxine Waters Floor Speech." (2003, March 18). [Video]. C-SPAN.

Hutchinson, L. (1973, January 30). "Yvonne Can't Kick the Barrier-Breaking Habit." *Chicago Tribune.*

Jordan, B. (1974, July 24). "'My Faith in the Constitution Is Whole; It Is Complete; It Is Total.'" Miller Center, University of Virginia.

Lee, B. (2006). *Renegade for Peace and Justice: Congresswoman Barbara Lee Speaks for Me.* Rowman & Littlefield.

Lee, B. (2018, August 15). "Happy birthday to my dear friend and sister in the struggle, Congresswoman Maxine Waters!" *Facebook.*

Leighton, S. (1965, March 7). "Congress' New Glamour Girl." *Pittsburgh Press.*

Lynch, S., Director. (2004). *Chisholm '72—Unbought and Unbossed.* [Documentary film.]

Marks, P. (2000, November 8). "The 2000 Elections: The Media; A Flawed Call Adds to High Drama." *New York Times.*

"1,000 Riot and Battle Police in Watts Area." (1965, August 12). *Los Angeles Times.*

Perlez, J. (2001, September 15). "US Demands Arab Countries Choose Sides." *New York Times.*

"President Trump Continues Attacking Maxine Waters after She Cancels Events over Death Threats." (2018, July 3). *Time.*

Queally, J. (2015, July 29). "Watts Riots: Traffic Stop Was the Spark That Ignited Days of Destruction in L.A." *Los Angeles Times.*

"'Reclaiming My Time': Rep. Maxine Waters Interrupts Mnuchin's Roundabout Answer." (2017, August 1). [Video]. *Washington Post.*

Rosenbaum, D. (2000, November 9). "State Officials Don't Expect Recount to Change Outcome." *New York Times.*

Sciolino, E. (2001, September 16). "Long Battle Seen." *New York Times.*

"Shirley Chisholm Speaking at Barbara Lee's California State Senate Victory Dinner." (1996). [Video].

Squires, J. (1973, February 6). "Barbara's Cold, Calculating, and Very Competent." *Chicago Tribune.*

Tolliver, J. (2023, September 9). "Interview with Representative Barbara Lee."

University of Michigan Department of History. (n.d.). "Model Minority." Deconstructing the Model Minority at the University of Michigan.

"Violence in the City—An End or a Beginning?" (1965). Governor's Commission on the Los Angeles Riots.

The National Visionary Leadership Project. (2010, April 27). "Shirley Chisholm: the First Black Congresswoman." [Video]. *YouTube.*

"Watts Rebellion (Los Angeles)." (n.d.). The Martin Luther King, Jr. Research and Education Institute at Stanford University.

"Watts Riots." (n.d.). Civil Rights Digital Library.

"What Patsy Mink Made Possible: Title IX at 50." (2022, August 26). National Women's History Museum.

Wu, J. T., and G. Mink. (2022). *Fierce and Fearless: Patsy Takemoto Mink, First Woman of Color in Congress.* NYU Press.

Wu, J. T., and G. Mink. (2022, June 1). "How Patsy Takemoto Mink, the First Woman of Color in Congress, Helped Craft Title IX." *Time.*

Chapter Nine: The Legacy

Apple Jr., R. W. (1972, June 24). "Three Black Leaders to Back McGovern." *New York Times.*

Apple Jr., R. W. (1972, July 7). "McGovern Shy 130 Votes as Delegate Choice Ends." *New York Times.*

Atske, S. (2024, April 23). "Misinformation and Competing Views of Reality Abounded Throughout 2020." Pew Research Center.

Chavda, J. (2024, April 14). "22 States Have Ever Elected a Black Woman to Congress." Pew Research Center.

Chisholm, S. (1973). *The Good Fight.* HarperCollins.

Frankel, M. (1972, July 11). "Majority is 1,618." *New York Times.*

Georgia Election Results 2018: Georgia Governor." *Politico.*

Goldsmith, A., and J. Newman. (2024, July 22). "A Look Back at Shirley Chisholm's 1972 Presidential Run, in Photos." *Town & Country.*

hooks, b. (1989). *Talking Back: Thinking Feminist, Thinking Black.* South End Press.

NBC News. (2022, November 5). "MTP75 Archives—Shirley Chisholm:

'I've Broken the Ice' Becoming the First Black Woman in Congress." [Video]. *YouTube.*

"North Carolina Election Results 2016: North Carolina Senate." *Politico.*

"North Carolina Election Results 2020: North Carolina Senate." *Politico.*

"North Carolina Election Results 2022: North Carolina Senate." *Politico.*

Norwood, C. (2023, December 18). "Cheri Beasley on the Promise, the Work and the Peril of Campaigning as a Black Woman." The 19th*.

"'Suppression': Critics Charge Georgia GOP Gov Candidate Purging Voters Before Election." (2018, October 11). NBC.

"Vice President Kamala Harris on Becoming 'Momala' to Her Husband's Kids: The Drew Barrymore Show." (2024, April 29). [Video]. *YouTube.*

Conclusion: The Power

"Attorney General Kamala D. Harris Urges Federal Courts to Protect." (2016, August 15). State of California—Department of Justice—Office of the Attorney General.

"Exchange Between Sen. Harris and Judge Kavanaugh on Mueller Investigation (C-SPAN)." (2018, September 6). [Video]. *YouTube.*

Galston, W. A. (2021, July 6). "New 2020 Voter Data: How Biden Won, How Trump Kept the Race Close, and What It Tells Us About the Future." Brookings.

Heimpel, D. (2015, March 9). "Kamala Harris' Bureau of Children's Justice Takes Shape." Goldman School of Public Policy at Berkeley University.

Jones, B. (2018, August 9). "An Examination of the 2016 Electorate, Based on Validated Voters." Pew Research Center.

Lopez, G. (2019, February 7). "Why Kamala Harris Is Under Attack for a Decade-Old Anti-truancy Program." *Vox.*

McKend, E. (2024, July 21). "Thousands of Black Women Join Call to Rally Around Harris." CNN.

Price, M. L., J. C. Smyth, L. Willingham, and B. Barrow. (2024, July 23). "JD Vance Slams Kamala Harris During His Solo Campaign Debut." AP News.

Rupin, A. (2024, July 22). "Harris Campaign Raises a Record $81 Million in 24 Hours." *Axios.*

Shabad, R., and J. Wu. (2024, July 21). "Which Democrats Are Calling on Biden to Step Aside? A Running List." NBC.

Singh, K. (2024, July 21). "Text of Biden Statement on Him Stepping Aside as Candidate." Reuters.

The Frost Tapes. (2020, October 6). Season 1, Episode 3.

"Trump Says Kamala Harris Was 'Extraordinarily Nasty' to Brett Kavanaugh." (2020, August 11). *Axios.*

Walker, H. (2019, January 22). "Kamala Harris Takes 'Responsibility' for Opposing Trans Surgeries." *Out.*

Wiggins, C. (2024, March 14). "Kamala Harris Reunites with Gay Couple She Wed 20 Years Ago." *Advocate.*

ACKNOWLEDGMENTS

I AM BEYOND GRATEFUL TO EVERY SINGLE PERSON WHO HAS encouraged me throughout this process, and who chooses to read this book. To my love, Leist, thank you for holding my hands, and wrapping me up in love and grace every day. I adore you. Thank you to my manager, Josanne Lopez, who knew that this story was in me the entire time. Thank you to the Legacy Lit team for seeing my vision and helping me bring this vivid story to life. To my writing coach and sister friend, Rachel Skerritt, thank you for all of your gentle nudges to stay the course, especially in my moments of doubt. To the researchers, archivists, writers, filmmakers, and storytellers who have chronicled Shirley Chisholm's humanity and her story, thank you for being a guiding light. Congresswoman Barbara Lee, thank you for openly sharing your experiences with me, and for planting the seeds of this story. I still can't believe that I am the first person to ask you for a follow-up interview about this once-in-an-era party. To my granddad, thank you for celebrating every milestone and every hurdle I've overcome. You have been a constant source of love and magic in my life, and I am forever grateful to you. Thank you to my parents for always believing in my big dreams. To my sisters, Diana, Kristen, and Ciara, and my niece, Amaya, I hope I make you proud. To my friends who listened to my hopes and aspirations, and encouraged me every step of the way—Charity, Stefanie, Missayr,

Sarah, Ariana, Ashley, Xiao, Tameisha, Wisambi Brionne, and Vernessa—you were my first readers and my inspiration. Thank you for seeing me. I have never considered myself to be someone who had a "team," but this project has shown me otherwise. I appreciate y'all more than you know.